Aimed at final year undergraduates and masters students, this is a new series of texts covering core subjects in Operational Research in an accessible student-friendly format. Each core subject will be paired with another core subject in order to provide maximum value for money for students.

The Operational Research series aims to provide a new generation of European-originated texts focusing on the practical relevance of those topics to today's students. To guarantee accessibility, the texts are concise and take a non-mathematical orientation in favour of software applications and business relevance. These texts provide students with the grounding in Operational Research they need to become the practitioners, users and innovators of tomorrow.

D1615356

5 141 907 6

Linear Programming
Mik Wisniewski

Critical Path Analysis
Jonathan H. Klein

palgrave

First published 2001 by
PALGRAVE
Houndmills, Basingstoke, Hampshire RG21 6XS and
175 Fifth Avenue, New York, N.Y. 10010
Companies and representatives throughout the world

PALGRAVE is the new global academic imprint of
St. Martin's Press LLC Scholarly and Reference Division and
Palgrave Publishers Ltd (formerly Macmillan Press Ltd).

ISBN 0–333–76354–8 hardback
ISBN 0–333–76355–6 paperback

This book is printed on paper suitable for recycling and
made from fully managed and sustained forest sources.

A catalogue record for this book is available from the
British Library.

Formatted by
The Ascenders Partnership, Basingstoke

10 9 8 7 6 5 4 3 2 1
10 09 08 07 06 05 04 03 02 01

Printed and bound in Great Britain by
Creative Print and Design (Wales), Ebbw Vale

Contents

Linear Programming

1   Introduction   3
    The structure of the text   5

2   Linear Programming: an introduction   7
    Business example   7
    Formulating the problem   8
    Solving an LP problem   10
    Interpreting the solution   16
    Simple sensitivity analysis   17
    Other types of constraint and objective function   24
    Solution to minimization problems   25
    Infeasible and unbounded problems   26
    Redundant constraints   28
    Summary   29

3   The Simplex method   30
    The Simplex formulation   30
    The Simplex solution process   31
    Summary of the Simplex method   40
    Extensions to the Simplex   41
    Minimization problems   48
    The dual problem   49
    Sensitivity analysis   56
    Summary   66

4   Linear Programming and computer software   67
    Microsoft Excel Solver   67
    XPRESS-MP   71
    Summary   75

5   LP in the real world   77
    Santos seaport, Brazil   77
    Brunswick Smelting, Canada   79
    Aluminium recycling, Saudi Arabia   82
    Summary   85

6   LP: where next?   **87**
Specialist LP applications   87
Development of other MP models   89
Algorithm development   91
Modelling and reporting developments   92
Conclusion   92

Bibliography   93

Exercises   96

Critical Path Analysis

7   Introduction   **107**
7.1 Projects   107
7.2 Characteristics of projects   110
7.3 An introductory example: planning and monitoring
     a research project   112
7.4 Structure of the text   117

8   Critical Path Network analysis techniques   **119**
8.1 Introduction   119
8.2 The critical path method   120
     8.2.1 Work breakdown structure (WBS)   121
     8.2.2 Precedence relationships   123
     8.2.3 Activity-on-node (AON) diagram   124
     8.2.4 Activity-on-arrow (AOA) diagram   126
     8.2.5 Activity timings   127
     8.2.6 Critical path   130
     8.2.7 Dummy activities   130
     8.2.8 CPM: concluding comments   132
8.3 The Gantt chart   132
8.4 Introducing duration uncertainty into network schedules   134
8.5 Trading off duration and cost   140
8.6 Resource usage   143

9   Critical Path Network software   **148**
9.1 Introduction   148
9.2 Commercial Critical Path network software   149
9.3 Critical Path Network applications on spreadsheets   155

10 Practical application **157**
10.1 Introduction 157
10.2 Critical Path Analysis and the life cycle of projects 158
10.3 The size and detail of projects 160
10.4 Critical Path Network approaches within organizations 163

11 A survey of Critical Path Methods literature **165**
11.1 Introduction 165
11.2 Introductory material 165
11.3 Specialized texts 166
11.4 Case studies and other material 167

12 Current issues in Critical Path Network analysis **168**
12.1 Introduction 168
12.2 Current issues in Critical Path Methods use 168
12.3 Conclusion 173

References 175

Exercises 179

List of figures

Linear Programming

2.1	Constraint 1	11
2.2	Feasible area	12
2.3	Objective function	14
2.4	Feasible area and objective function	15
2.5	Optimal solution	15
2.6	Sensitivity analysis: objective function	22
2.7	Minimization	26
2.8	Infeasibility	27
3.1	Simplex solutions	34
3.2	Surplus variables	43
4.1	Microsoft Excel Solver template	68
4.2	Spreadsheet set-up	68
4.3	Formulae	69
4.4	Solver details	69
4.5	Solution	70
4.6	Sensitivity analysis	71
4.7	XPRESS-MP model builder	72
4.8	XPRESS-MP optimizer dialogue box	73
4.9	Results dialogue box	74
4.10	Model errors	75

Critical Path Analysis

7.1	Gantt chart (or schedule graph) for the consulting project	114
8.1	A word breakdown structure for the EBSP Detector Project	122
8.2	An activity-on-node (AON) diagram for the EBSP Detector Project	125
8.3	An activity-on-arrow (AOA) diagram for the EBSP Detector Project	127

8.4 Activity-on-arrow diagram for the EBSP Detector
     Project   129
8.5 A dummy activity is used to distinguish between
     activities B and C   131
8.6 Activity D must be preceded by both of activities
     A and B, but activity C need only be preceded by
     activity A   131
8.7 The EBSP Detector Project displayed as a Gantt chart   133
8.8 Illustrations of the Beta probability distribution   135
8.9 Activity-on-arrow diagram for the EBSP Detector
     Project with revised data   138
8.10 The Normal probability distribution   139
8.11 The Gantt chart of Figure 2.7, with activity C2
     reduced by one day   141
8.12 A minimum time schedule Gantt chart for the
     EBSP Detector Project   142
8.13 Latest time schedule for the EBSP Detector Project   145

List of tables

Linear Programming

Tableau 1	32	Tableau 5	44
2	33	6	45
3	38	7	46
4	39	8	47

Tables
3.1	Primal solution: Tableau 4 reiterated	51
3.2	Dual solution	51
3.3	Dual solution: minimization problem	55
3.4	Tableau 4 and its Simplex solution reiterated	57
3.5	Tableau 4 with RHS adjustments	58
3.6	Simplex solution with constraints taking the form ≥	60
3.7	Optimal Simplex solution with additional product	64
3.8	Basic variable B	64
3.9	Basic variable D	65
E1	Raw materials for Exercise 5	97
E2	Exercise 7: 4-stage production process	98

Critical Path Analysis

7.1	Component activities for the consultancy project	113
8.1	Activities for the EBSP Detector Project	123
8.2	Activity durations and precedence relationships for the EBSP Detector Project	125
8.3	ES, LS, EF and LF times, total and free slack, and critical path status for the activities of the EBSP Detector Project	129
8.4	Most likely, optimistic and pessimistic estimates for the activities of the EBSP Detector Project	137
8.5	Probability of completion by various dates for the EBSP Detector Project	139

8.7 Normal and crash durations, and costs of duration reductions, for activities C1, C2, C3 and C4 in the EBSP Detector Project 140

8.8 Activity reductions to derive a minimum time schedule for the EBSP Detector Project 142

8.9 Cost profiles for earliest time (ET) and latest time (LT) schedules for the EBSP Detector Project 146

Linear Programming

Mik Wisniewski

1 Introduction

What do the following situations have in common?

- The Arabian Light Metals Company (ALMC) is the largest producer of aluminium bars in Kuwait. The bars are used by local industry to produce aluminium doors, windows and sheeting for kitchens and bathrooms. The company has around 35 per cent of the domestic market but is facing increasing competition from foreign manufacturers. The bars are made from a mixture of pure materials and recycled materials. Some of the recycled supply comes from the company's own manufacturing process. A second source is the metal scrap market in Kuwait where scrap aluminium can be bought. The combination of pure and recycled materials has to be carefully controlled to ensure appropriate quality of the final product. There is a finite supply of recycled material. There is also a finite demand for this product in Kuwait. The company is keen to control its costs and increase its profitability. It is trying to decide on the appropriate quantities of pure metals and recycled scrap to be used in production that will keep its costs to a minimum and at the same time meet the required quality standards.

- Health service planners in Rome are trying to plan the home-care service provided to AIDS patients. The service includes medical care and social care support. The public sector organizations providing such care must work within fixed budgets and within existing staff levels. They are expected to meet, or exceed, minimum standards in terms of the care provided. However, there is uncertainty over the future number of patients who will need such care service and over the type and amount of care that any individual patient will require. The planners are trying to ensure that the maximum number of patients receive care to the standards required but within the limits of existing budgets and staffing levels.

- The US airline company, Delta Air Lines, has around 2500 domestic flights to organize each day with some 450 aircraft of

3

different types and sizes available. If one of the company's aircraft takes off with empty seats this represents lost revenue. On the other hand, aircraft which take off full, leaving passengers behind who could not get a seat, also represent lost revenue. Assigning the right aircraft type to the right flights is therefore critical but increasingly difficult given uncertainties over passenger demand. The company is trying to ensure it maximizes the revenue earned from passengers whilst keeping its operating costs as low as possible.

These situations have several features in common.

The first is that they all relate to problems common to many businesses, public and private sector alike, large or small, manufacturing or service. The second is that, although the exact details of the situation will naturally vary from one organization to another, these situations all relate to problems where management are trying to determine the *best* solution to the problem. Thirdly, the search for the best solution is *constrained* by very specific requirements of such a solution. Delta, for example, are constrained in their search for increased revenue by the maximum number of aircraft they have available. The Rome planners are constrained by the maximum number of staff available. ALMC is constrained in that its production has to meet specified quality requirements. The last thing these situations have in common is that the technique of *linear programming* (LP) has been successfully applied to them all. In the case of the ALMC, not only was LP used to find the best solution in terms of the mix of metals required, but the technique was estimated to have resulted in annual net savings for the company of almost US$2m. Delta estimates that the application of LP saved some US$300m over a three-year period.

Linear programming is one of a family of quantitative models known as *mathematical programming* models. These models – of which LP was the first to be developed and is still the most commonly applied – all involve searching for some optimum solution (and hence are also often referred to as optimization models). The search for an optimum is more usually described as searching for a maximum or a minimum, depending on the exact problem. So, for example, we may be searching for maximum profit, or minimum cost, or maximum number of patients to be treated. In LP terminology the maximization/minimization of some quantity is referred to as the *objective*. All these optimization models also involve searching for an optimum quantity under certain restrictions or *constraints* that limit the extent to which the objective can be pursued. The models are generically referred to as *mathematical* programming models because we must describe the business problem we are examining in mathematical terms. That is, the objective and the problem constraints must all be expressed mathematically. For LP, such expressions must also be *linear* in form. This means that they can be shown on a graph as a straight line.

LP was developed in the 1940s. Over the last decade or so, it has seen a resurgence in popularity, thanks in large part to the rapid development of desktop computer processing power. The solution of a large LP problem requires considerable computing power and, until fairly recently, the cost and availability of this restricted applications of LP to a relatively small number of application areas and to those organizations which could afford the computer power required. Now, however, large LP problems can be readily solved using spreadsheets and this makes them available to many more managers and decision-makers searching for an optimum solution to a decision problem. A cursory search of the World Wide Web in July 2000 using LP as the keywords revealed over 40 000 web pages. Equally, managers have realized the added value of LP through what is known as *what-if analysis*. Such analysis – readily undertaken as part of an LP solution – allows a manager to assess the effect on the optimum solution of a range of possible decisions. *What would happen to the number of patients I could care for if we took on more staff? What would happen to costs if we acquired extra aircraft? What would happen to our costs if we altered the quality requirements of our products?* These are the sort of 'what-if' questions of considerable interest to managers and the sort of questions that LP is good at answering.

The structure of the text

In Chapter 2 we introduce the basic formulation of an LP problem and see how such a problem can be solved using a graphical approach. We also see how 'what-if' information can be generated from the solution. In Chapter 3 we develop the LP solution approach further using what is known as the Simplex method. This solution method can be applied to any LP problem of any size and is the solution approach typically used by specialist LP computer programs. In Chapter 4 we see how LP problems are solved using computer software and we illustrate the approach and the solution output using two typical programs. In Chapter 5 we examine a number of case studies to see how LP is actually applied in practice and consider some of the practical problems involved. Finally, in Chapter 6, we consider some of the developments in and around LP to assess the directions in which LP is moving.

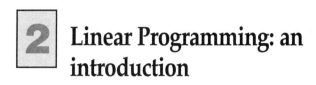

2 Linear Programming: an introduction

In this chapter we introduce the basic linear programming model and develop the graphical method as a means of finding an optimal solution to an LP problem. Typically, all LP problems have two common features: they involve some declared objective which we seek to optimize (looking for either a maximum or minimum value depending on the exact problem) and they involve a set of constraints which limit the way in which we can attain this objective. The formulation of a business problem into an LP format is almost an art form in its own sake requiring not only a familiarity with the technique itself but also familiarity with the business problem. Fortunately, the solution of an LP problem once formulated is much more straightforward: we use appropriate computer software to find the solution for us. To begin with, however, we examine a more mundane solution process based on graphs. This method is particularly useful as an introduction to LP solution as it facilitates an understanding of the concepts of the technique and its solution algorithm. Such an understanding is essential before we introduce a more complex solution method.

Business example

We shall develop our understanding of LP with a simple business example. A clothing company manufactures two versions of denim jeans: a basic pair (B) and a fashion design pair (D). It is trying to determine how many of the two products to manufacture. The manufacturing process is largely automated and the company buys in bulk supplies of denim cloth. The jeans are manufactured in a two-stage process. In the first stage the denim cloth is cut to a standard pattern. For the basic jeans, B, this process takes three minutes per pair and for the design jeans, D, it takes six minutes. After cutting, the jeans then go through the second stage where the cut cloth is sewn together, zips are sewn in and the company's logo patch sewn on the back pocket of the jeans. This stage takes eight minutes for each pair of B and four minutes for each pair of D. The jeans are then sold to high street retailers at a standard price of £39.90 for B and £44.90 for D. The company estimates that it actually costs £34.90 to produce a pair of B and £38.40 to produce a pair of D. The company has several machines available for each stage of the process. On a typical day the cutting machines used in stage one are available for a total of 80 hours 30 mins and the sewing machinery for a total of 86 h and 40 mins. The company's logo patches which are sewn onto each pair of jeans are limited in supply, coming from an outside manufacturer who can only supply 1200 each day. The same logo patch is used for both B and D. Both products are currently selling well, and effectively the company can sell as many of these items as it can manufacture. The production manager faces a basic decision: *how many of each product should be produced each day?*

Formulating the problem

There are two stages in formulating the business problem into an LP format: deriving an *objective function* and deriving *constraints*.

The objective function

The first step is to clarify what the manager is trying to achieve. The logical objective in this situation would be to seek to maximize the profit achieved from the two products. Under certain conditions we might instead wish to maximize sales revenue or minimize production costs. The key words we have used here are *maximize* and *minimize* and one or the other is always to be found in an LP application. We assume that the manager wishes to maximize profit. We can then express the profit relationship in mathematical terms. With the two products B and D we know the costs and the selling price per unit so can derive the profit per unit as £5 for each pair of B jeans (£39.90 – £34.90) and £6.50 for each pair of D jeans (£44.90 – £38.40). In mathematical terms we then have:

$$\text{Profit} = 5B + 6.5D$$

where B is the number of pairs of basic jeans produced and D is the number of design jeans produced. The function shows the profit the company will make for any combination of output. This is known as the *objective function* (OF). It is important to note that mathematically the function is linear – it involves variables no higher than power 1 and will give us a straight line on a graph. At first sight it might appear that the manager should concentrate production on D since this has a higher per unit profit contribution. However, this does not take into account the limitations we face on production in terms of the available machine time and the number of logo patches available. Somehow we must incorporate this information. B and D are usually referred to as the *decision variables*, since it is these variables we require some decision on in terms of their optimum numerical values.

Constraints

The limitations that we face – there are three in this problem – are more generally known as *constraints*. They literally constrain, or restrict, us in terms of what we can and cannot do to achieve profit. For example, it is not possible to produce 800 units of each product per day because from one constraint we know we only have 1200 patches available, hence total production must be limited to a maximum of 1200 of both products per day. Quite simply, we are constrained from producing more than 1200 items. (You may also have worked out that this combination of production would also violate the other two constraints in terms of available machine time.) We can express the patch constraint mathematically as:

$$1B + 1D \leq 1200$$

Combined production, $1B + 1D$, must be less than or equal to 1200. The constraint relating to the cutting process can be determined in the same way. The total machine time available is 4830 mins each day (the 80 h 30 mins availability shown as total minutes). This represents the maximum time available. Each unit of B requires 3 of these minutes whilst each unit of D requires 6 mins. We then have:

$$3B + 6D \leq 4830$$

Similarly, the third constraint is:

$$8B + 4D \leq 5200 \text{ (the 86 h 40 mins shown as total minutes)}$$

indicating the maximum sewing time available and the time required for all combinations of B and D.

Problem formulation

We can now bring together the parts of our problem into a formal problem formulation. We seek to maximize profit subject to the various constraints faced. We have:

$$\text{Max. } 5B + 6.5D$$

subject to:

$$1B + 1D \leq 1200$$
$$3B + 6D \leq 4830$$
$$8B + 4D \leq 5200$$

$$B, D \geq 0$$

We shall refer to this formulation as Problem A. The last expression – often referred to as a *non-negativity constraint* – has been added to indicate that negative values for B and D are not permitted (obviously they do not make sense in the context of the problem). This is the standard method of presenting an LP problem formulation. It sets out clearly our objective and our constraints. Note that once again the constraints are linear in format.

Solving an LP problem

In this section we shall introduce a solution method based on graphs. Whilst this is a little cumbersome and awkward it will help us understand how the solution process works. Later we shall introduce a more detailed and general solution method.

Graphing the constraints

First, we shall graph the constraints for the problem. Let us examine the first constraint:

$$1B + 1D \leq 1200$$

We know the constraint indicates maximum production in the context of available logo patches. Suppose we decided to produce zero units of B. This would mean that the maximum possible production of D was 1200. Similarly, if we produced zero D then maximum B would be 1200. We then have two co-ordinates for our graph:

$$(0, 1200) \text{ and } (1200,0)$$

Consider Figure 2.1 with D on the vertical axis and B on the horizontal (it would not matter if we did it the other way round). The two sets of co-ordinates are marked on the two axes and represent maximum possible productions in the context of this one constraint. By joining these two points together with a straight line (since the relationship for the constraint is linear) we show all the other maximum production possibilities. The line of the constraint represents a *production possibility frontier*. To illustrate this consider the production combinations:

1. B=400, D=400
2. B=400, D=800
3. B=400, D=1000

which are also shown on Figure 2.1. We see that Point 1 is below the constraint line, Point 2 is actually on the line whilst Point 3 is above the line. Consider these positions in the context of this constraint. We know that maximum production is 1200 units. Point 1 is for total production at 800 units – below the production frontier. Point 2 is for exactly 1200 units – actually on the frontier. Point 3 is for 1400 units – beyond the frontier. In the vocabulary of LP we would note Points 1 and 2 as being *feasible* – they are possible given the constraint. Point 3 on the other hand is *infeasible* – it cannot be

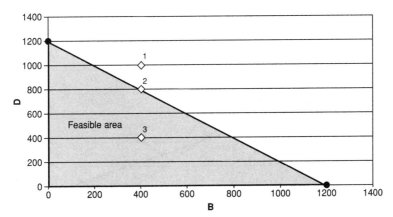

Figure 2.1 Constraint 1

attained given the constraint. The area below the constraint line (including the actual line itself) would be our feasible area – it shows all the feasible combinations of production for this constraint. The area above the line would be the infeasible area – those combinations of production which were unattainable for this constraint.

Adding other constraints

The other two constraints can be added to the diagram in the same way:

- Setting B=0 find D
- Setting D=0 find B
- Using these co-ordinates plot both points on the graph
- Join the two points together to form the production frontier
- Identify the new feasible area.

The co-ordinates would be:

Constraint 2: 0,805 and 1610,0
Constraint 3: 0,1300 and 650,0

Figure 2.2 shows the second and third constraints added. The feasible area shown indicates the production possibilities that are feasible for all constraints simultaneously. Any combination of production that falls into the feasible area is possible given all the

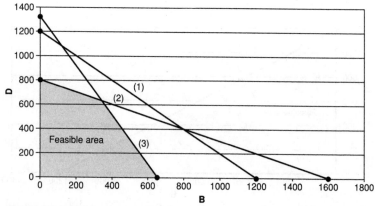

Figure 2.2 Feasible area

constraints. But which of these possibilities represents maximum profit? The answer is that we do not yet know, for we have not yet incorporated the objective function into the diagram.

Graphing the objective function

Recollect that our objective function is:

$$5B + 6.5D$$

and that we wish to add this to the graph of the feasible area. You might see that we have a difficulty because in our OF we have neither an equation or an inequality. There is no right hand side value in the function against which to work out values for B and D. We can get round this problem – and examine the characteristics of the function – by choosing an arbitrary value for profit. For example, suppose we set profit at £1300. With zero units of D then we must produce:

$$\frac{1300}{5} = 260 \text{ units of B to achieve this profit}$$

and similarly with B=0, then D=200 would also give a profit of £1300. We now have two sets of co-ordinates for our graph:

(260,0) and (0,200)

and as before we can plot these points on a graph and join them together with a straight line. Anywhere along the line we are achieving a profit of exactly £1300. Such a line is often referred to as an *iso*-line joining points of an equal numerical value, in this case it is technically known as an iso-profit line. Our choice of profit – at £1300 – was arbitrary. We could have chosen any numerical value. Figure 2.3 shows three iso-profit lines, for £1300, £3900 and £6500. There are a number of points we can make. The first is that all the lines are parallel – mathematically they have the same slope. This must be the case because they all show the relative profitability of B to D and this does not change. The second point is that the lines move upwards and outwards away from the origin the higher the profit becomes. Given our objective of profit maximization then we would seek to be on the line representing the highest profit. Here it would be the line furthest from the origin. In principle, you should realize that although we have drawn only three lines here we could

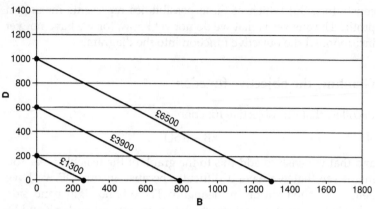

Figure 2.3 Objective function

have drawn an infinite number, with each representing a different profit. We seek to be on the highest – the one furthest from the origin. What will stop the manager from moving to an ever-higher profit line is the feasible area. This shows us the area in which we must remain, given the constraints imposed.

Finding an optimal solution

We are now at a point where we can find the solution to our problem. Graphically we wish to be on the highest possible profit line. The feasible area, however, will limit how high the line can be since we must remain in the feasible area at all times. Consider Figure 2.4. This shows the feasible area and the three iso-profit lines. We see that all the lowest line – for £1300 – is entirely within the feasible area. This implies that any production which generates £1300 profit is feasible. With the next line – £3900 – part falls in the feasible area and part outside. Some combinations of production which give rise to this profit are feasible whilst others are not. With the third line all combinations are infeasible indicating that a profit of £6500 is unattainable given these constraints.

Recollect that these are just three of the many profit lines that could have been drawn. It is clear that as we move from one line to another – upwards and to the right – less and less of the line will fall in the feasible area. We wish to move onto as high a profit line as possible and yet must still remain in the feasible area. There will

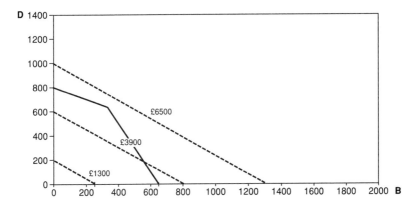

Figure 2.4 Feasible and objective function

come a time when there is only one point – literally – on the profit line that is also in the feasible area. This is shown in Figure 2.5. We see that the profit line shown just coincides with the corner point of the feasible area. The next higher profit line will leave the feasible area altogether – and hence is not attainable. The lower profit line is of no interest given the objective function. This point, therefore, is the optimum solution – the combination of output which leads to the highest possible profit given the constraints imposed on the problem. We see from the graph that this represents 330 units of B and 640 units of D. Note that the solution has occurred at one of the

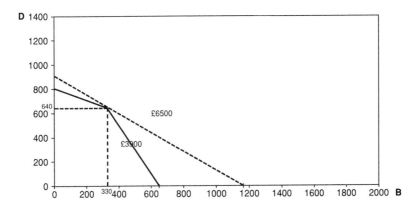

Figure 2.5 Optimal solution

corner points of the feasible area. This is typically where the optimal solution will be found.

Solution procedure

Let us summarize the solution procedure that we have developed so far.

1. Formulate the problem into an objective function and set of constraints.
2. Plot each constraint on a graph by setting each variable in turn to zero and solving for the other to find the co-ordinates.
3. With all constraints on the graph outline the feasible area common to all constraints. Locate the corner points of the feasible area.
4. Choose an arbitrary – but sensible – value for the objective function. Setting each variable in turn to zero solve for the other to find the co-ordinates.
5. Plot this function on the graph.
6. Since all the objective functions will be parallel we can use this single function to determine the optimal point.
7. For a maximization problem we seek to push the objective function as far from the origin as possible. From the feasible area identify visually which of the corner points the OF line will intercept last as it moves away from the origin.
8. This point will be the optimum solution.
9. From the graph determine the values of the two variables at this point.

Normally the solution to an LP problem will be found at one of the corner points of the feasible area. We need, therefore, to draw only one OF line to determine which of these corner points it will be.

Interpreting the solution

It is always important not just to find the numerical solution but to be able to interpret the solution in the context of the business problem. Recollect that we were seeking to help the production manager determine the optimum daily production. We have found that this should be:

330 pairs of B jeans

640 pairs of D jeans

from the OF we know this will generate a daily profit of:

$$5(330) + 6.5(640) = £5810$$

In terms of the constraints we will require:

$$330 + 640 = 970 \text{ logo patches}$$

and you will recollect that maximum supply was 1200. Of the available cutting time we will require:

$$3(330) + 6(640) = 4830 \text{ mins}$$

and there are 4830 mins available. Of the available sewing time we will require:

$$8(330) + 4(640) = 5200$$

and again there were 5200 mins available. Not only have we found the optimum solution for the production manager's problem, we have also gained an insight into the resources required. As far as machine time is concerned – both cutting and sewing – we are using all the available resources to generate the profit maximizing level of production. There is excess supply, however, of the third resource – the available logo patches. We shall see in later sections how this information can be used by the manager.

Simple sensitivity analysis

We have seen how we find the solution to an LP problem. In this section we consider how we can extend the information we can extract from the solution that will be of help to the manager in the decision making process. The production manager will be interested in this optimal solution since it indicates the mixture of production that will maximize profit. However, the manager is also likely to be interested in obtaining other relevant information about the problem. The manager may well pose the question:

I now know what my maximum profit will be given the existing constraints. What should I do to try to generate more profit?

This is known as sensitivity analysis, since we examine how sensitive the solution is to changes in its formulation. It is also referred to as 'what-if' analysis. We have already established that at the optimal solution we will require:

> 970 patches (with 1200 available)
> 4830 mins of cutting time (with 4830 available)
> 5200 mins of sewing time (with 5200 available)

Consider this information from the manager's viewpoint. We know that all the available machine time for both cutting and sewing is required to maximize profit. However, we do not require all the available patches. There is some spare capacity (230 to be precise). In the context of LP we would describe the two constraints relating to machine time as *binding* constraints. At the optimal solution they prevent us from achieving more profit since we have exhausted the supply of these resources. On the other hand the constraint relating to patches is *non-binding*. At the optimal point we could produce more output in the context of this one constraint since we still have supplies of this resource available. We shall soon see that this distinction between binding and non-binding constraints is important. From Figure 2.2 we see that the optimal point falls *on* the lines of the two machine time constraints. It falls *below* the constraint line for patches. This implies that the demand for this resource – at the optimal solution point – is less than the available supply. We have some spare patches in other words. What this means is that we can determine directly from the graph which constraints are binding and which are not. Those lines on which the optimum point falls represent binding constraints. Other lines are non-binding.

Non-binding constraints indicate surplus resources. The company does not actually need 1200 patches per day. This may enable the manager to reduce costs by cutting back on resources which are not actually needed. Binding constraints indicate scarcity. We have exhausted the supply of that resource at the optimal point. It will be worth the manager's while to examine possible increases in the supply of such scarce resources to determine whether this would lead to even more profit. In short, the manager might ask:

> *I know I have no more machine time for cutting currently available. But if I bought an extra machine – and hence increased supply beyond 4830 mins – could I earn more profit?*

We shall return to this question shortly.

Solution through simultaneous equations

It will probably have occurred to you that finding the solution through a graph is a somewhat clumsy – and potentially inaccurate – method. We can verify our solution using simultaneous equations. Our original problem formulation expressed the constraints as inequalities. At the optimal solution we now know that two constraints are binding. This implies that these two constraints can be rewritten as:

$$3B + 6D = 4830$$
$$8B + 4D = 5200$$

since we know – at the optimal solution – the demand for each of these resources exactly matches the supply. In effect we can now say that we seek the solution values for B and D to these two equations – we want the values that satisfy both equations simultaneously. Finding the solution to these two equations through simultaneous equations gives $D = 640$ and $B = 330$, confirming our graphical solution. There are two aspects to sensitivity analysis that we can now explore. The first is to examine the constraints. The second is to examine the objective function.

Sensitivity analysis on the constraints

As we have established, it is the fixed supply of certain resources that is restricting the profit the company can achieve. We have noted that the two machine time constraints are binding – they are both having a directly restrictive effect on profit at the optimal solution. Suppose the manager asked the question: *what would happen if we made more machine time available for cutting?* Increasing the supply would – in principle – allow us to produce more and thereby make more profit. The difficulty is that we cannot be precise about how much extra production and how much extra profit. However, consider the following scenario. Assume that – somehow – we can increase the supply of machine time for cutting by 1 min. This follows what is known as a *marginal* approach and is particularly important in sensitivity analysis. The two binding constraints would then be:

$$3B + 6D = 4831$$
$$8B + 4D = 5200$$

(the objective function and the third constraint are unchanged).
Clearly we would expect a marginal change in the solution. In
graphical terms the constraint line would be pushed outwards from
its current position to indicate a marginally increased supply of this
resource and hence the feasible area would also change marginally.
It is evident that graphically it would be impossible to assess the
impact of such a marginal change. Using simultaneous equations,
however, we can readily determine the new solution.
The new solution is:

$$B = 329.8888$$
$$D = 640.2222$$
$$\text{Profit} = £5810.89$$

We see that there has been a marginal change in the solution.
Production of B has gone down slightly, that of D has gone up and
there has been a slight increase in profit as a result. The manager
now knows that increasing the machine time for cutting by 1 min
will lead to an increase in profit of £0.89. From the original formulation the manager is now thinking of making extra time available for
sewing. The problem now becomes:

$$3B + 6D = 4830$$
$$8B + 4D = 5201$$

with a solution:

$$B = 330.1667$$
$$D = 639.9167$$
$$\text{Profit} = £5810.29$$

To illustrate the use of such information assume that the manager
knows that cutting time and sewing time cannot both be increased.
Which should be prioritized? Clearly, if we cannot increase both we
should prioritize the one which will generate most profit, other
things being equal, since this is our objective after all. This is cutting
time which adds an extra 89 pence per minute to profit. The extra
profit, 89p for cutting time and 29p for sewing, is often referred to
as the *opportunity cost* of the binding constraints (also as the *shadow
price* or the *dual value*). The opportunity cost refers to the cost of *not*
doing something. Here, the cost of not acquiring extra cutting time
is 89p per minute in terms of lost profit. Such opportunity costs
allow the manager to prioritize between scarce resources. The

opportunity cost of the non-binding constraint could be worked out using simultaneous equations but in fact there is no need. The non-binding constraint relates to patches. We are effectively posing the question: *how much will profit increase if we obtain an extra supply of patches?* The answer is: profit will not change. We already have more than we need – the definition of a non-binding constraint. Increasing the supply will not allow us to produce more of the two products. You will see that any non-binding constraint will have a zero opportunity cost whilst any binding constraint will have some positive opportunity cost.

One aspect of this investigation that we are unable to resolve at this stage relates to the quantity of the extra resource. Clearly one extra minute of cutting time is ridiculous. We would want an hour or a day – more than a minute. The question is: *how many minutes are worthwhile in an opportunity cost sense?* We will have to wait until the next chapter before we can answer this.

Sensitivity analysis on the objective function

In much the same way we might want to carry out sensitivity analysis on the objective function. We have found the solution only in terms of the existing profit contributions of the two products. If either of these contributions changed then were might expect a change in the optimal solution. However, it would be tedious to have to recalculate the solution every time there was some minor change in profit contributions. Sensitivity analysis seeks to establish the maximum change that can occur in one of the objective function coefficients before the solution changes. Consider product B. This currently has a profit contribution of £5. If this changed to, say, £5.10 it is unlikely to have much, if any, effect on the optimal solution. On the other hand if it changed to, say, £15 then we might expect a change in the optimal mix of production. We are seeking an answer to the question: *how much could the profit contribution of B change without affecting the profit maximizing combination of outputs?* Recollect the approach we took in the graphical solution. We set an arbitrary level for the objective function in order to be able to draw it on the graph. We did this in order to establish the slope or gradient of the profit line. We noted that for different profit levels the slope of all the lines would be the same. This is because the slope of the profit line indicates the relative profitability of the two products.

Consider Figure 2.6. This shows the current profit line. If B's profit contribution increased and D's remained unchanged then the line would pivot around its current position as shown. To generate the same profit we need produce fewer units of B, given it is now more profitable per unit. If B had become less profitable the line would pivot in the opposite direction. Recollect that the optimal point is found by determining which of the corner points of the feasible area we encounter last as the profit line moves outwards. The slope of the profit line will, in part, determine which corner point this will be. If the slope of the profit line changes so much then the optimum corner point will change (and so will the solution in terms of the mix of production). Clearly, we could repeat this analysis for product D and its profit contribution. To generalize, consider Figure 2.5 which showed the feasible area and the current OF line. The OF could pivot in several ways depending on the relative profitabilities. There are, however, limits to this movement if we are to remain at the current solution point. If the line pivoted too much we would move to a new solution point on the B axis. Clearly this would happen if B became so profitable that we gave up production of D altogether. Equally, if B's profit contribution fell sufficiently we would move to a new solution point on the D axis. You will be able to see that neither of these will happen as long as the slope of the OF line is between the slope of the two binding constraints. Consider the binding constraint:

$$3B + 6D = 4830$$

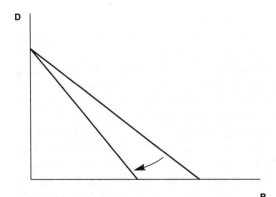

Figure 2.6 Sensitivity analysis: objective function

We can rearrange to give:

$$3B + 6D = 4830$$
$$6D = 4830 - 3B$$
$$D = \frac{4830 - 3B}{6} = 805 - 0.5B$$

that is, this line has an intercept of 805 and a slope of -0.5.

The second binding constraint is:

$$8B + 4D = 5200$$
$$4D = 5200 - 8B$$
$$D = \frac{5200 - 8B}{4} = 1300 - 2B$$

giving a slope of -2. We now know that as long as the slope of the OF line is between -0.5 and -2 then the optimal solution will remain the current one. If the slope of the line changes outside these limits the optimal solution will change also. The slope of the existing profit line is:

$$\text{Profit} = 5B + 6.5D$$

Rearranging gives:

$$6.5D = -5B$$
$$D = \frac{-5}{6.5}B = -0.769B$$

with a slope of -0.769 which falls between the two limits set. However, as we established earlier if the profit contribution of either of the two products changes then the slope of the line will change. Suppose the profit contribution of B changes to £5.50. The slope of the new profit line is then:

$$B = \frac{-5.5}{6.5}B = -0.846$$

Since this is still within the limits set (-0.5 to -2) this indicates that the current solution will not alter (although of course the company will make more profit from its current production). We can go one step further and establish what the precise maximum limits are. Let us consider B. We require:

$$-2 \le -\frac{\text{profit contribution of B}}{6.5} \le -0.5$$

Using the left-hand inequality this requires:

$$-2 \leq -\frac{\text{profit contribution of B}}{6.5}$$

or $-13 \leq -\text{profit contribution of B}$

or   profit contribution of B ≤ 13.

In other words as long as the profit contribution of B is below £13 the slope of the profit line will not exceed –2. On the right hand side we have:

$$\frac{-\text{profit contribution of B}}{6.5} \leq -0.5$$

or $-\text{profit contribution of B} \leq -3.75$

or   profit contribution of B ≥ 3.75

Again, as long as the profit contribution of B is greater than £3.75 the slope of the profit line will be less than -0.5. In other words, as long as the profit contribution of B is between £3.75 pence and £13 the current solution will remain optimal (based on the assumption that D's contribution has remained the same). Think about the advantages this gives the production manager who now knows that they can plan for production on the basis of 330 units of B and 640 units of D per day as long as the profit margin of B is between these two limits. If the marketing department are planning to increase the selling price of B then the production manager can readily determine whether this will affect the optimal production mix. Naturally, we can repeat this analysis for D. Using the same logic we have:

$$-2 \leq \frac{-5}{\text{profit contribution of H}} \leq -0.5$$

and this gives an equivalent range between £2.50 and £10.

Other types of constraint and objective function

In our example, we have assumed we wished to maximize profit subject to maximum supplies of certain resources (machine time and logo patches). We may also face problems where we wish to minimize some function. In our example we may wish to *minimize* total production costs for example. LP is just as happy with a minimizing objective function as with a maximizing. Equally, our constraints have all been of the type ≤, indicating a maximum value which cannot be exceeded. In some problems we may have constraints indicating a minimum value which *must* be exceeded. For example, assume the company has received an order for 300 pairs of D jeans. This would take the form of ≥ constraint. On some occasions we might also insist on a strict equality (=), perhaps we have a contract to supply a customer with exactly 200 pairs of D and 300 of B. Again, these types of constraint are easily incorporated. As an example, assume the production manager has now decided to minimize total costs rather than maximize profit. Additionally, production of D must be at least 300 units and total production at least 750 units. The three original constraints still apply. The problem then becomes:

$$\text{Min. } 34.9B + 38.4D$$

subject to:

$$1B + 1D \leq 1200$$
$$3B + 6D \leq 4830$$
$$8B + 4D \leq 5200$$
$$1D \geq 300$$
$$1B + 1D \geq 750$$

$$B, D \geq 0$$

Solution to minimization problems

The solution of minimization problems is effectively the same with the exception of step 7 in the procedure we summarized earlier. For minimization problems we seek as *low* a value for the OF as possible. This implies that we want to push the OF line as close to the origin as possible – rather than as far away as possible as in a maximization problem. Returning to the minimization problem that we have just formulated, the solution is shown in Figure 2.7 with the feasible area marked. Note that the ≥ constraints imply the feasible area is beyond the line (away from the origin) rather than below as is the case with ≤ constraints. The OF line has been added to identify its slope – it really does not matter where this line is (that is, what value for the OF you have arbitrarily selected). We see that

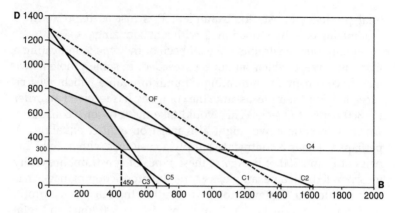

Figure 2.7 Minimization

as we force the line inwards – closer and closer to the origin – the last corner point of the feasible area that we encounter will be the point marked on the graph. This gives a solution of:

$$B = 450$$
$$D = 300$$
$$Costs = £27\,225$$

which is the cost minimizing production given the constraints. The interpretation for the rest of the problem implies that:

    450 patches will remain unused
    1680 mins of cutting time will remain unused
    400 mins of sewing time will remain unused

whilst we are meeting the two $\geq$ constraints exactly. Production of D is 300 – the minimum required – and total production is 750 also the minimum required. We could also complete exactly the same sort of sensitivity analysis on this solution as we did for our earlier maximization problem. This is left as an exercise.

Infeasible and unbounded problems

Not all LP problems will actually have a solution. There are two types of situation where this may occur.

Infeasibility

The first situation occurs when a problem is infeasible – it is impossible to satisfy all the constraints simultaneously and therefore no feasible area actually exists.

Returning to the initial problem we looked at, that of profit maximization, suppose we added a further constraint. We have had an order for 650 pairs of B and 700 pairs of D.

$$\text{Max. } 5B + 6.5D$$

subject to:

$$1B + 1D \leq 1200$$
$$B + 6D \leq 4830$$
$$8B + 4D \leq 5200$$
$$B \geq 650$$
$$D \geq 700$$

$$B,D \geq 0$$

Figure 2.8 shows that we have one area satisfying the first three constraints and a second area satisfying the last two. But we have no area which satisfies all constraints simultaneously, hence no solution exists. In the real world, recognizing infeasibility can be important to management. It indicates that an organization's planned activities are not deliverable. Further analysis of the problem can also provide management information on what needs to be done to create a feasible solution.

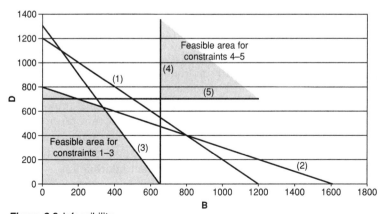

Figure 2.8 Infeasibility

Unbounded problems

The second situation occurs when a problem is unbounded. An unbounded problem occurs where the OF can take infinitely large values without violating any of the constraints. An unbounded problem occurs in practice when the problem has not been properly formulated: some critical constraint has been omitted. Whilst this will be obvious in the small problems we have examined so far, in practice this can be difficult to identify at the formulation stage. It is only when a solution to the formulation is sought that management will realize some critical constraint factor has not been taken into account.

Redundant constraints

Finally, we must mention the issue of *redundant* constraints. Again, in the small problems we have examined, the issue of redundancy is not a real problem. In practice, however, it can be very problematic. A redundant constraint is one which does not affect the feasible area and can be removed from the formulation without affecting the optimal solution. Returning to our profit maximization problem, suppose each pair of jeans was packed into a plastic bag before shipping to customers. We have 1500 of these bags available on a daily basis. The constraint then becomes:

$$1B + 1D \leq 1500.$$

However, given that we already have the logo patch constraint at:

$$1B + 1D \leq 1200$$

then the plastic bag constraint is redundant. Any solution which satisfies the logo patch constraint (that is, a combined production of no more than 1200) must automatically satisfy the plastic bag constraint. In large problems, identification and removal of redundant constraints can significantly reduce the time taken to find a solution. However, we need to be cautious about removing redundant constraints. Sometimes sensitivity analysis on redundant constraints can highlight useful management information.

Summary

In this chapter we have introduced the basic LP model, its formulation, its solution and interpretation and sensitivity analysis. In the next chapter we shall extend our analysis to allow us to examine larger and more realistic LP problems.

3 The Simplex method

We have seen how the graphical solution method can be used to find the optimal solution to a two variable LP problem and how we can carry out sensitivity analysis. Clearly, in a business environment, we will never be faced with such a simple problem so in this chapter we introduce a general-purpose solution method, known as the Simplex method. An understanding of the principles of the Simplex method is important since most computer based LP packages use this approach. Without this understanding, it will be difficult to understand how solutions are determined and how the output from such packages can properly be interpreted.

The Simplex formulation

Recollect that for our basic profit maximization problem that we used in Chapter 2 the formulation is:

$$\text{Max. } 5B + 6.5D$$

subject to:

$$1B + 1D \leq 1200$$
$$3B + 6D \leq 4830$$
$$8B + 4D \leq 5200$$

$$B, D \geq 0$$

Although we already know the optimal solution, we shall use the Simplex method to confirm this. The Simplex method is a solution process that iteratively solves sets of equations until an optimal solution is found. We must first transform constraint inequalities into equations.

Introducing slack variables

Consider the first constraint:

$$1B + 1D \leq 1200$$

We can rewrite this as:

$$1B + 1D + 1S_1 = 1200$$

where the new variable, S_1, is known as a *slack* variable. A slack variable is introduced into the Simplex formulation to transform an inequality of the form ≤ into an equation. It measures the difference between the left-hand side of the constraint and the right hand side for particular combinations of B and D. Suppose we had:

$$B = 100, D = 200$$

We know from the constraint that we will then require 300 logo patches although 1200 are available. In the equation S_1 must be 900 – the difference, or slack, between the resources required and those available. For any combination of values for B and D, therefore, S_1 will simply indicate the spare resources relating to that constraint. Note that conventionally we denote the slack variable for the first constraint with the subscript $_1$. Constraint 2 would become:

$$3B + 6D + 1S_2 = 4830$$

and constraint 3:

$$8B + 4D + 1S_3 = 5200$$

giving a complete formulation of:

$$\text{Max. } 5B + 6.5D$$

subject to:

$$1B + 1D + 1S_1 = 1200$$
$$3B + 6D + 1S_2 = 4830$$
$$8B + 4D + 1S_3 = 5200$$

$$B, D, S_1, S_2, S_3 \geq 0$$

The slack variables do not appear in the objective function in the formulation. They have no contribution to make to profit.

The Simplex solution process

We now have a set of 3 equations involving 5 variables and we seek a solution to this equation set. You will be aware that when we have more variables than equations it is not possible to find a unique solution to a set of equations. But we said earlier the Simplex method solves sets of equations. If we have more variables than equations and cannot find a unique solution what can we do? The answer is that we set some of the variables to zero and solve for the remainder. By doing this for different combinations of variables we will produce different solutions and we can compare each solution in terms of the value for the objective function that it generates. As usual this sounds more complicated than it is. We will find that, in practice, the Simplex method follows a set of simple 'rules' – which of course makes it very suitable for solution using a computer.

The Simplex tableau

In order to progress we must first introduce the method of representing each solution in the form of a table – or tableau. This is the common method of showing the various stages of the Simplex process. The initial tableau represents our formulation:

Tableau 1

	B	D	S_1	S_2	S_3	Value
OF	5	6.5	0	0	0	0
Constraint 1	1	1	1	0	0	1200
Constraint 2	3	6	0	1	0	4830
Constraint 3	8	4	0	0	1	5200

The rows of the tableau represent, respectively, the Objective Function (OF) and the constraints. The columns represent the variables – the decision variables first followed by the slack variables. The coefficients in the tableau are taken from the formulation. If, for example, we look at the third row this actually represents the equation:

$$3B + 6D + 0S_1 + 1S_2 + 0S_3 = 4830$$

Note that the OF takes a value of zero. With no production there can be no profit.

First iteration

In order to find a solution to the equation set we must set some of the variables to zero and solve for the remainder. With 3 equations and 5 variables we must set 2 variables to zero. With a total of 5 variables there are a number of combinations that we could set to zero. The Simplex method, however, always starts in the same way. It sets the decision variables to zero – B and D. Whilst we would not regard this as very sensible, since only B and D contribute to profit, it has some logic for the Simplex in that it always starts us from the worst possible point. Anything we do after this must be an improvement. Profit will clearly be zero since output is zero. We will also have the following values for the slack variables:

$$S_1 = 1200$$
$$S_2 = 4830$$
$$S_3 = 5200$$

that is, all the resources are slack, or unused. Fig. 3.1 shows our problem with the current solution at the origin, where both B and D are zero. We must now transform our tableau to represent this solution. This is easily done.

Tableau 2

	B	D	S_1	S_2	S_3	Value
OF	5	6.5	0	0	0	0
S_1	1	1	1	0	0	1200
S_2	3	6	0	1	0	4830
S_3	8	4	0	0	1	5200

All that has changed are the labels of the last three rows. These – and the corresponding values on the right hand side of the row – now represent the slack variables. If we look at the S_1 row we have:

$$1B + 1D + 1S_1 = 1200$$

Since B and D are zero this means that we really have:

$$1S_1 = 1200$$

This type of tableau will now be what we see at each stage. The rows will indicate the variables for which solution values have been found – these are known as *basic* variables. Variables which do not appear in the tableau – here B and D – are known as *non-basic* variables and take a value of zero. The tableau indicates the values that these basic variables take – 1200, 4830 and 5200 respectively – and the value of the objective function – here 0. Having found a basic solution we now seek to determine whether we can improve this solution in the context of the objective function. In terms of the Simplex, having found a solution at one corner point of the feasible area we now seek to determine whether another – and adjacent – corner point would be a better solution. The Simplex method only looks for adjacent corner points to the current solution – that is, corner points which are next to the current solution in terms of the boundary of the feasible area. In Figure 3.1 we are at Point I. As far as the Simplex is concerned the adjacent corner points are Points II and III. Point IV is not regarded as adjacent to Point I since we cannot reach it directly – we must go through Point II or III first. Consider what this implies. If we move towards Point II we are moving along the D axis. Given that D is currently zero this means that D will take some positive value as we move towards Point II. The value of the OF will increase. The other adjacent corner point is Point III. This implies moving along the B axis and with the same logic the OF will also increase. Other things being equal we would want to move along the D axis since D contributes £6.50 to profit as against £5 for B. The question now arises: *how can we tell this from the Simplex tableau?* Let us examine the OF row in Tableau 2. We see that the D column has a coefficient of 6.5 and the B column a coefficient of 5 (all other columns are zero). The interpretation is straightforward. Introducing D into the solution will increase the OF by 6.5 per unit, whilst B will increase the OF by 5. Our decision rule, therefore, would be to bring into the solution the variable with

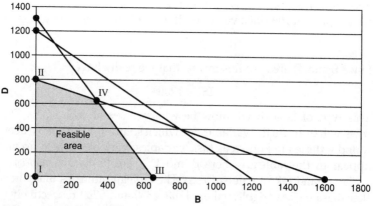

Figure 3.1 Simplex solutions

the highest positive coefficient in the OF row (negative coefficients would imply that the OF would decrease in value). However, as we have seen, we still have only three equations. If we wish to bring in D (that is, to give D a non-zero value) then one of the existing basic variables must leave the tableau to make room. In the jargon of LP, one of the currently basic variables must become non-basic – it must be set to zero.

The next question, therefore, is which one – S_1, S_2 or S_3? Again let us examine the graph. We wish to move along the D axis. In terms of our constraints we will have to stop when we 'bump' into constraint line 2. We cannot move further up the axis without leaving the feasible area. Again, how can we tell this from the tableau? Let us focus on the D column in the tableau (since D is the variable entering the solution). Each unit of D will require:

1 patch (with 1200 available)
6 minutes of cutting time (with 4830 available)
4 minutes of sewing time (with 5200 available)

Some simple arithmetic, therefore, indicates:

$$\frac{1200}{1} = 1200$$

$$\frac{4830}{6} = 805$$

$$\frac{5200}{4} = 1300$$

as the maximum possible production of D in the context of each individual constraint and accordingly each represents the intercept of that constraint on the D axis. Clearly we must take the smallest of these ratio results – here at 805 – to determine the furthest point along this axis that we can move. This ratio corresponds to the S_2 row in the tableau. We now state that, since D is entering the solution, S_2 must leave. At the next stage, therefore, S_2 will become non-basic and by definition will take a zero value. Consider what this means. S_2 represents the slack resources in terms of constraint 2. If S_2 is zero it means that there is no slack – we are using all the resource in production. This must be the case since at Point II this constraint will be binding. So our next solution point will be at Point II. We must now transform the tableau to represent this point since clearly the current values will change.

Transforming the tableau

We do this through a number of simple steps.

1. Identify the pivot column. This we have already done by choosing column D.
2. Identify the pivot row. Again we have also done this by calculating ratios and choosing the smallest. This is row S_2.
3. The intersection of pivot column and row indicates the pivot element. This will be 6.
4. Transform the current pivot row by dividing through by the pivot element.
5. Transform the existing rows by using the new D row.

Taking the current row we have:

$$3B + 6D + 0S_1 + 1S_2 + 0S_3 = 4830$$

and dividing by 6 gives:

$$0.5B + 1D + 0S_1 + 0.1667S_2 + 0S_3 = 805$$

Consider what we have now achieved. At the next solution point, B is still non-basic and takes a value zero. S_2 will now also be non-basic and take a value zero. Hence the expression we have just derived actually simplifies to:

$$D = 805$$

In other words, we have 'solved' for D. But by moving to a different corner point of the feasible area the existing tableau – Tableau 2 – will no longer be appropriate since this is the tableau for the previous corner point. The next step, therefore, is to transform the existing tableau to represent the new corner point. We have already done this for row 3 – S_2 being replaced in the basis by D. The other rows must be changed also.

The new D row provides a general expression for the units of D produced. We see that from Row 2 – S_1 – and the D column that each unit of D requires 1 unit of S_1. Recollect that S_1 represents unused patches. So, for every unit of D we produce we will need one of our unused patches. We will obviously need to calculate the number of unused patches that will be left after we have produced the current output of D – 805 units. This is determined – and the new S_1 row obtained – through a simple calculation.

1. We take the existing S_1 row.
2. We take the new D row and multiply it by the coefficient corresponding to the S_1 row and the pivot column (D). Here, this coefficient is 1.
3. We subtract the result in step 2 from step 1. This gives the new S_1 row.

S_1	1	1	1	0	0	1200
$-D \times 1$	-0.5	-1	0	-0.1667	0	-805
S_1	0.5	0	1	-0.1667	0	395

and the result is the new S_1 row. S_1 – unused patches – has now fallen to 395. This is entirely logical since we are producing 805 units of D, we have 1200 patches in total hence (1200–805) 395 will be unused. We can repeat this process for the two remaining rows – S_3 and OF. The new S_3 row will be:

S_3	8	4	0	0	1	5200
$-D \times 4$	-2	-4	0	-0.6667	0	3220
S_3	6	0	0	-0.6667	1	1980

giving S_3=1980 at the new solution point. Recollect that we had 5200 mins of sewing time. Each unit of D requires 4 mins (hence the multiplication by 4 above). We are producing 805 units of D and therefore require 3220 mins of sewing time in total. The new OF row is found in exactly the same way.

OF	5	6.5	0	0	0	0
$-D \times 6.5$	-3.25	-6.5	0	-1.0833	0	-5232.5
OF	1.75	0	0	-1.0833	0	-5232.5

The new OF value will be –5232.5. This seems a little odd when we remember that the OF shows the profit achieved. We know that the profit should be £6.50 × 805 or £5232.50. This is one of the odd things about the way the Simplex method works. The value for the OF actually has the wrong sign – it should read positive not negative. We must reverse the sign in each tableau. It is worth noting that many LP computer programs will reverse the sign automatically for you. So our new tableau will be:

Tableau 3

	B	D	S_1	S_2	S_3	Value
OF	1.75	0	0	−1.0833	0	−5 232.5
S_1	0.5	0	1	−0.1667	0	395
D	0.5	1	0	0.1667	0	805
S_3	6	0	0	−0.6667	1	1 980

representing a solution where:

$$\text{Profit} = £5232.50$$

$$B = 0$$
$$D = 805$$

$$S_1 = 395$$
$$S_2 = 0$$
$$S_3 = 1980$$

It is important to understand the logic of variables moving into and out of the current solution tableau. Computer solutions to LP follow the same process and without such an understanding it will be difficult to assess the information such computer packages provide.

Subsequent iterations

Although the process we have just completed may seem complicated all we have actually done is to follow a set of simple steps. All we do from now on is to repeat these for our new tableau. Before we do this, though, consider Figure 3.1. We are currently at Point II and have moved from Point I. The Simplex method will now ascertain whether a move to an adjacent corner point would represent an improvement in the Objective Function. The obvious one is Point IV, but there is also Point I – the point we have just left. (Point III is not adjacent and cannot be considered at this stage.) The first thing is to choose the pivot column. We see from the OF row that only two columns have non-zero values: B and S_2. This is logical since we have just determined that there are only two adjacent corner points. Let us consider S_2 ,with a coefficient of −1.0833. S_2 represents unused cutting time. If we were to force $S_2>0$ then we are effectively insisting on having unused cutting time. The

only way this can be achieved at the moment is to cut back on D
production (since this is currently using all the available time). This
will move us back in the direction of Point I. The effect on profit –
the OF – will be to reduce profit by 1.0833 for each minute (unit) of
S_2 that we insist on having. This is not something we would
logically choose to do but it does illustrate an important point about
the Simplex tableau. Every part of the tableau tells us something
about the current problem and we must ensure we are able to
interpret the coefficients correctly in the context of the problem and
the current stage of the solution process. However, it will be more
instructive to consider the other coefficient, 1.75 for B. This indicates that if we introduce B into the solution then the value of the
OF will rise by £1.75 for each unit of B that we introduce. In other
words we are being told that at this stage it will be profitable to
produce units of B in addition to units of D. The rest of the Simplex
process is now as before. The pivot row is found by taking the
current variable values and dividing through by the coefficients in
the pivot column. This gives:

$$S_1 \quad \frac{395}{0.5} = 790$$

$$D \quad \frac{805}{0.5} = 1610$$

$$S_1 \quad \frac{1980}{6} = 330$$

We choose the smallest of these, 330, to give the pivot element of 6.
This means that B is to enter the basis whilst S_3 is to leave (and take
a zero value). In other words, there will be no unused sewing time –
this constraint will be binding. Using this pivot element we can
transform the new S row by dividing the existing S_3 row by 6 to give:

B 1 0 0 –0.1111 0.1667 330

and this new B row can be used to transform the rest of the tableau.

Tableau 4

	B	D	S_1	S_2	S_3	Value
OF	0	0	0	–0.8889	–0.2920	–5810
S_1	0	0	1	–0.1111	–0.0833	230
D	0	1	0	0.2222	–0.0833	640
B	1	0	0	–0.1111	0.1667	330

We have:

> Profit = £5810 (remember to reverse the sign)
>
> B = 330
> D = 640
>
> $S_1 = 230$
> $S_2 = 0$
> $S_3 = 0$

Current production is 330 units of B and 640 units of D giving a profit of £5810. There are 230 unused patches and no unused machine time (constraints 2 and 3 are binding). The Simplex process now starts again from the beginning. In fact, we can only carry out the first stage. On examining the tableau we see that in the OF row there are only negative coefficients to be found. Consider what this implies. We know we are at Point IV where there are two adjacent corner points that we could move to. But the Simplex tableau indicates that if we were to do so the value of the OF would decline (the meaning of the negative coefficients). In other words we recognize that when there are no further positive coefficients in the OF row we must have reached the optimum solution.

Summary of the simplex method

Let us summarize the Simplex method as we have developed it so far.

1. Introduce slack variables into the formulation to transform the inequalities into equations.
2. Produce the initial formulation tableau.
3. Transform this tableau into the first solution by setting all decision variables to zero and allowing all slack variables to take their maximum values.
4. Identify the pivot column by locating the largest positive coefficient in the OF row.
5. Identify the pivot row by calculating the ratios of values to coefficients in the pivot column and choosing the smallest positive coefficient.

    The pivot column indicates the currently non-basic variable that is set to enter the basis.

The pivot row indicates the currently basic variable that is set to leave the basis.

The pivot element is the coefficient common to the pivot column and pivot row.

6. Divide the pivot row by the pivot element to obtain the new row coefficients.
7. Use this new row to adjust all existing rows and produce a new tableau.
8. Go back to step 4 until there are no further positive coefficients in the OF row. This is the optimal solution.

Extensions to the Simplex

In this section we shall introduce a number of extensions to the Simplex method to allow us to deal with other types of LP problems. Our problem is as before but we add two further constraints: minimum production of B must be 350 units and minimum total production must be 750 units. Clearly we can transform this into a Simplex formulation by adding slack variables to each of the first three constraints as before. But what about the two new constraints which are of the form ≥? Recollect the interpretation of a slack variable – it represents that amount of the resource that is unused given the current values of the decision variables. That is, the shortfall between the amount of the resource required on the left-hand side of the constraint from that available on the right hand side. As we have seen the slack variable could be zero – implying that all the resource is required – or it could be positive indicating that the left-hand side is less than the right. But consider the fourth constraint:

$$1B \geq 350$$

The left-hand side can never be less than the right so it makes no sense to talk of a slack variable for this constraint. Instead we introduce an equivalent: the *surplus* variable. This represents for this type of constraint the amount by which we *exceed* the minimum value required. In other words if we were to produce more than 350 units of B there would be a surplus, otherwise the surplus will be zero. We shall use the symbol SU together with a subscript to indicate a surplus variable and which constraint it relates to. We then have:

$$1B = 350 + 1SU_4$$

Notice that we have had to put the surplus variable on the right hand side since B must be 350 plus whatever value the surplus variable takes. We see that if SU_4 is zero then B must be exactly 350, whilst if $SU_4 > 0$ then B>350. It will be more convenient to move SU_4 to the other side of the equation to give:

$$1B - 1SU_4 = 350$$

Similarly, the last constraint will be:

$$1B + 1D - 1SU_5 = 750$$

and our formulation will then be:

$$\text{Max. } 5B + 6.5D$$

subject to:

$$1B + 1D + 1S_1 = 1200$$
$$3B + 6D + 1S_2 = 4830$$
$$8B + 4D + 1S_3 = 5200$$
$$1B - 1SU_4 = 350$$
$$1B + 1D - 1SU_5 = 750$$

$$B, D, S_1, S_2, S_3, SU_4, SU_5 \geq 0$$

We can treat the surplus variables in exactly the same way as slack variables in the Simplex solution process.

The initial solution

You will remember that the initial solution for the Simplex was found before by setting the decision variables to zero and solving for the remaining (slack) variables. With B and D both zero we then require:

$$S_1 = 1200$$
$$S_2 = 4830$$
$$S_3 = 5200$$

$$SU_4 = -350$$
$$SU_4 = -750$$

The surplus variables must take negative values in order to balance the corresponding equations. But in our formulation we have said that we cannot allow *any* variable to take a negative value. You may

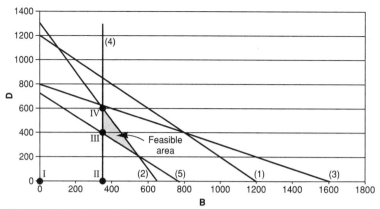

Figure 3.2 Surplus variables

see how we have got ourselves into this problem by examining Figure 3.2. We start the Simplex solution process from the origin – where B and D are zero. But for this problem – or indeed any problem involving $\geq$ constraints – the origin is not part of the feasible area. So we are actually trying to find a non-feasible solution. The Simplex method helps us out of our difficulty by introducing yet another type of variable.

Artificial variables

We introduce into each of the $\geq$ constraints an *artificial* variable. Such a variable has no real meaning in the problem but allows the Simplex method to work when we are trying to find a non-feasible solution. We add an artificial variable, A, to the fourth constraint:

$$1B - 1SU_4 + 1A_4 = 350$$

For the last constraint we have:

$$1B + 1D - 1SU_5 + A_5 = 750$$

to give a formulation of:

$$\text{Max. } 5B + 6.5D$$

subject to:

$$1B + 1D + 1S_1 = 1200$$
$$3B + 6D + 1S_2 = 4830$$

$$8B + 4D + 1S_3 = 5200$$
$$1B - 1SU_4 + 1A_4 = 350$$
$$1B + 1D - 1SU_5 + 1A_5 = 750$$

$$B, D, S_1, S_2, S_3, SU_4, SU_5, A_4, A_5 \geq 0$$

We now have 5 equations but 9 variables so 4 must be set to zero. What we can now do to find an initial solution is to set the decision variables to zero but also set the surplus variables to zero (since they were the ones causing the problems with negative values). We would now require:

$$S_1 = 1200$$
$$S_2 = 4830$$
$$S_3 = 5200$$
$$A_4 = 350$$
$$A_5 = 750$$

and with B,D,SU_4,SU_5 all zero we are not violating the formulation. However, we stress again that the artificial variables in such a problem have no real meaning. They are a device to allow the Simplex method to work when we have surplus variables which would take (unpermitted) negative values. As we shall see, the artificial variables will 'disappear' from the problem once they have served their purpose. The rest of the Simplex process, once we have included artificial variables, follows similar lines as before. The actual arithmetic involving the OF is a little more complicated to deal with the artificial variables. However, we need not go into the detail here. Instead, let us follow the logic by examining the tableau shown below, which relates to the initial formulation solution.

Tableau 5

	B	D	S_1	S_2	S_3	SU_4	SU_5	A_4	A_5	Value
OF	2005	1006.5	0	0	0	0	0	-1000	-1000	-1100000
S_1	1	1	1	0	0	0	0	0	0	1200
S_2	3	6	0	1	0	0	0	0	0	4830
S_3	8	4	0	0	1	0	0	0	0	5200
A_4	1	0	0	0	0	-1	0	1	0	350
A_5	1	1	0	0	0	0	-1	0	1	750

With the exception of the OF row you will see that each row represents one of the constraints in the original problem formulation. The current solution is:

$$B = 0$$
$$D = 0$$

$$S_1 = 1200$$
$$S_2 = 4830$$
$$S_3 = 5200$$

$$SU_4 = 0$$
$$SU_5 = 0$$

$$A_4 = 350$$
$$A_5 = 750$$

That is, the decision variables and the surplus variables have been set to zero whilst the remaining variables – including the artificial take their maximum values to satisfy the constraints. Note that the reason the OF looks different from the formulation is that we must use a special procedure when dealing with artificial variables. We need not concern ourselves with this since it is taken care of by the computer program we use to solve such an LP problem. Consider now the tableau for this problem for the next iteration.

Tableau 6

	B	D	S_1	S_2	S_3	SU_4	SU_5	A_4	A_5	Value
OF	0	1 007	0	0	0	1 005	−1 000	−2 000	0	−398 250
S_1	0	1	1	0	0	1	0	−1	0	850
S_2	0	6	0	1	0	3	0	−3	0	3 780
S_3	0	4	0	0	1	8	0	−8	0	2 400
B	1	0	0	0	0	−1	0	1	0	350
A_5	0	1	0	0	0	1	−1	−1	1	400

The solution and tableau are slightly more complicated than those we have examined so far, but exactly the same principles apply. We have:

$$B = 350$$
$$D = 0$$

$$S_1 = 850$$
$$S_2 = 3780$$
$$S_3 = 2400$$

$$SU_4 = 0$$
$$SU_5 = 0$$
$$A_4 = 0$$
$$A_5 = 400$$

In terms of our decision variables we are producing 350 units of B (the absolute minimum required). This then implies that we have spare resources – relating to the first three constraints – as shown by S_1, S_2 and S_3. Since we are producing the absolute minimum of B required by the formulation then the associated surplus variable – SU_4 – is zero. But, since we are producing the minimum of B required we no longer need the artificial variable for that constraint A_4, hence it can be set to zero (and will remain so for the rest of the solution process). However, we are still some way short (400 units) of producing the minimum output required for the last constraint, hence we still have A_5 which also indicates by how much we are short of satisfying this constraint. This solution corresponds to Point II on Figure 3.2, which has moved us towards the feasible area although we are still not on the feasible area boundary. The solution for the next iteration is then:

Tableau 7

	B	D	S_1	S_2	S_3	SU_4	SU_5	A_4	A_5	Value
OF	0	0	0	0	0	−1.5	6.5	−1 000	−1 000	−4 350
S_1	0	0	1	0	0	0	1	0	−1	450
S_2	0	0	0	1	0	−3	6	3	−6	1 380
S_3	0	0	0	0	1	4	4	−4	−4	800
B	1	0	0	0	0	−1	0	1	0	350
D	0	1	0	0	0	1	−1	−1	1	400

The interpretation follows as before.

$$\text{Profit} = £4350$$
$$B = 350$$
$$D = 400$$
$$S_1 = 450$$
$$S_2 = 1380$$
$$S_3 = 800$$

$$SU_4 = 0$$
$$SU_5 = 0$$
$$A_4 = 0$$
$$A_5 = 0$$

We are producing 350 units of B, 400 units of D and generating a profit of £4350. This combination of output meets *both* the ≥ constraints and so we no longer need either of the artificial variables. For the first time we have a solution which is feasible and puts us at Point III in Figure 3.2. The rest of the solution can be interpreted in the usual way. From now on the solution process proceeds exactly as before. The next variable to enter the basis will be SU_5 since this has the highest positive coefficient in the OF row. The next tableau will be as follows.

Tableau 8

	B	D	S_1	S_2	S_3	SU_4	SU_5	A_4	A_5	Value
OF	0	0	0	0	−1.63	−8	0	−992	−1000	−5650
S_1	0	0	1	0	−0.25	−1	0	1	0	250
S_2	0	0	0	1	−1.5	−9	0	9	0	180
SU_5	0	0	0	0	0.25	1	1	−1	−1	200
B	1	0	0	0	0	−1	0	1	0	350
D	0	1	0	0	0.25	2	0	−2	0	600

This solution is:

$$\text{Profit} = £5650$$
$$B = 350$$
$$D = 600$$
$$S_1 = 250$$
$$S_2 = 180$$
$$S_3 = 0$$
$$SU_4 = 0$$
$$SU_5 = 200$$
$$A_4 = 0$$
$$A_5 = 0$$

We are producing 350 units of B and 600 units of D to generate a profit of £5650. Note that this is lower than the profit for our original problem. By introducing the two additional constraints we are effectively reducing profit. The production manager should examine this and determine whether the minimum production requirements are absolutely necessary. We have spare patches (250) and spare cutting time (180 mins) but no spare sewing time. This last constraint is binding. There is no surplus production of B (SU_4 =0) hence this constraint is also binding. There is surplus production in terms of the minimum production requirement of 750 units (SU_5=200 since total production is 950). The two artificial variables are zero. We see that the solution is optimal since there are no positive coefficients in the OF row at this stage. The solution puts us at Point IV on the graph. We cannot introduce a new variable and increase profit further.

Equality constraints

Our final type of constraint is that requiring a strict equality. Suppose the last constraint in the previous problem had been:

$$1B + 1D = 750$$

that is, we require a production of exactly 750 units. This might relate, for example, to an existing contract we have to supply exactly this amount. It is evident that in such a case there will be no slack but equally no surplus. The two sides of the constraint must always balance. It will also be evident that graphically the solution must be exactly on the line of this constraint. The feasible area, therefore, will only occur on this constraint line. We will then face the same problem as before in trying to apply the Simplex to infeasible solutions. We have, however, the same solution. We can introduce an artificial variable for such a constraint until we encounter a feasible solution in the Simplex process.

Minimization problems

With minimization problems, we saw that graphically they pose no problems. We seek to push the OF line as close to the origin as possible. A similar adjustment is needed here for the Simplex method. Given we are seeking the lowest possible value for such an objective function when we are deciding which variable should enter the basis, we would now choose the one with the *smallest* coefficient in the OF row rather than the largest. Otherwise the Simplex method proceeds as before.

The dual problem

We saw in Chapter 2 that sensitivity analysis has an important part to play in LP. In this section we introduce the dual problem which provides the theoretical basis for such sensitivity analysis.

The primal and dual relationship

The problems we have formulated and solved are technically known as *primal* problems. For any such primal problem there exists a comparable problem known as the *dual* which is effectively a mirror image of the primal and has important consequences for sensitivity analysis. To develop the relationship between primal and dual problems we shall return to the principle of opportunity costs established in Chapter 2 with Problem A. You will recollect that the opportunity cost could be interpreted as the value of an extra unit of a resource. The opportunity cost of cutting time would indicate the extra profit that could be achieved if we were able to acquire extra supplies of this resource over and above those needed at the optimal solution. Each resource (represented by a constraint) will have such an opportunity cost (although of course the value of the opportunity cost will vary from constraint to constraint). We shall denote these opportunity costs as U_1, U_2 and U_3 for each of our three resources. Since there is an available supply of 1200 patches it follows that the maximum price the company will be willing to pay for this supply would be:

$$1200 \times U_1$$

that is, the supply multiplied by the per unit opportunity costs. The firm would not be willing to pay more since the value of the total supply is indicated by the opportunity cost – the total effect on the objective function, profit. For the other two resources we have:

$$4830U_2$$

and

$$5200U_3$$

So, the total amount the company would be willing to pay for all of these resources would be:

$$1200U_1 + 4830U_2 + 5200U_3$$

Logically the company will want to minimize this total payment. However, there will be restrictions – constraints – on how the company can minimize this payment. These constraints will relate to the resources required to produce the two products. Each unit of B requires:

> 1 patch
> 3 mins of cutting time
> 8 mins of sewing time

so the maximum value of these resources to the company will be:

$$1U_1 + 3U_2 + 8U_3$$

But these resources will be used to produce 1 unit of B and thereby generate a profit of £5. The value of the resources to the company must be worth at least the profit earned so we have:

$$1U_1 + 3U_2 + 8U_3 \geq 5$$

Using similar logic for D we have:

$$1U_1 + 6U_2 + 4U_3 \geq 6.5$$

where again the resources used produce 1 unit of D at a profit of £6.5. So we actually have a problem where we require:

Minimize:

$$1200U_1 + 4830U_2 + 5200U_3$$

subject to:

$$1U_1 + 3U_2 + 8U_3 \geq 5$$
$$1U_1 + 6U_2 + 4U_3 \geq 6.5$$

$$U_1, U_2, U_3 \geq 0$$

This formulation is known as the *dual* of the original problem. It is evident that both the primal and dual formulations are directly related since they both use the same coefficients (although in different ways). It is not yet clear what purpose the dual problem serves. In fact the relationship between the primal and dual and the uses of the dual become apparent once we solve the dual and compare that solution to the primal. Shown below is the Simplex solution to the primal problem that we developed earlier in Tableau 4.

Table 3.1   Primal solution: Tableau 4 reiterated

	B	D	S_1	S_2	S_3	Value
OF	0	0	0	−0.8889	−0.2920	−5810
S_1	0	0	1	−0.1111	−0.0833	230
D	0	1	0	0.2222	−0.0833	640
B	1	0	0	−0.1111	0.1667	330

The solution to the dual formulation is:

Table 3.2   Dual solution

	U_1	U_2	U_3	SU_1	SU_2	Value
OF	230	0	0	330	640	−5810
U_3	0.0833	0	1	−0.1667	0.0833	0.292
U_2	0.1111	1	0	0.1111	−0.2222	0.8889

In both cases the OF takes a value of £5810. We also see that the solution values that we had in the primal appear in the OF row of the dual and *vice versa*. Clearly there are very strong similarities between the two. In fact there are three key properties of the primal-dual relationship which we state without proof.

Property 1

If the primal problem has an optimal solution (that is, there is a feasible solution) then the dual has an optimal solution. The objective function values of the two optimal solutions are the same. As we have seen both OF values are £5810.

Property 2

In the dual optimal solution the coefficients in the OF row are the optimal values for the slack variables and the decision variables of the primal problem. So, from the dual solution we have:

Dual	U_1	U_2	U_3	SU_1	SU_2
	230	0	0	330	640
Primal	S_1	S_2	S_3	B	D

So we obtain identical values – and solutions – for all parts of the problem from either the dual or the primal solutions.

Property 3

The optimal values for the dual decision variables are the opportunity costs for the corresponding constraints in the primal problem.

This is the last – and potentially most important – property of the primal-dual relationship. You will remember the issue of sensitivity analysis in the context of a graphical solution from Section 2. We have not yet been able to explore sensitivity analysis – important though it is – in the context of the Simplex solution. This third property will allow us to do so. For example U_3 – we said – is the opportunity cost of the third resource, sewing time. From the dual solution this gives a value of 0.292. Consider the OF in the dual:

$$5810 = 1200U_1 + 4830U_2 + 5200U_3$$

$$= 1200(0) + 4830(0.8889) + 5200(0.292)$$

$$= 5810$$

Suppose we increase the supply of sewing time by one minute, to 5201. We can then calculate the new OF value for the dual. This will be:

$$OF = 1200U_1 + 4830U_2 + 5201U_3$$

$$= 1200(0) + 4830(0.8889) + 5201(0.292)$$

$$= 5810.292$$

That is, the OF increases by 29.2 p because of this extra minute of sewing time made available. But through property 1 this change in the dual OF value must also bring about the same change in the OF value of the primal. An extra minute of sewing time will, therefore, bring about an increase in profit (the primal OF) of 29.2 p. Recollect this was the exact interpretation of the opportunity cost in Chapter 2. From the dual we have:

$$U_1 = 0$$
$$U_2 = 0.8889$$

Since the maximum supply of patches is not used at the primal solution (S_1=230) then the opportunity cost is zero. Acquiring extra patches will not affect profit. For cutting time the opportunity cost is 88.89 p per min.

Transforming the primal to the dual

In our simple problem it was relatively straightforward to transform the primal into the dual. For more complex primal problems a number of straightforward transformation rules can be applied. We shall illustrate with reference to the more complex problem we have examined:

Primal formulation

$$\text{Max. } 5S + 6.5D$$

subject to:

$$1B + 1D \leq 1200$$
$$3B + 6D \leq 4830$$
$$8B + 4D \leq 5200$$
$$1B \geq 350$$
$$1B + 1D \geq 750$$

It will be necessary to change the primal into what is known as the *canonical* primal. Such a primal is always a maximization formulation and involves only constraints taking the form ≤. The canonical primal can then be transformed into the corresponding dual which will always be a minimization problem and involve only constraints taking the form ≥. You will see that the current primal formulation is not in canonical primal format.

Transformation rules for a canonical primal

Constraints taking the form ≥

A constraint taking the form ≥ can be transformed for the canonical primal by multiplying through by −1. This turns it into a constraint of the form ≤. We have:

$$1B \geq 350$$

and

$$1B + 1D \geq 750$$

These become:

$$-1B \leq -350$$

and

$$-1B - 1D \leq -750$$

Constraints taking the form =

Suppose our last constraint had actually been:

$$1B + 1D = 750$$

It must take the form ≤ in order to meet the requirements of the canonical primal formulation. This appears difficult given that we require a less-than constraint but actually have an equality. We can require the same restriction by having two constraints:

$$1B + 1D \leq 750$$

and

$$1B + 1D \geq 750$$

Naturally, the only situation that will satisfy both these constraints is to have 1B+1D exactly equal to 750. The second of these, of course, must also be transformed using the previous rule above.

Objective functions involving minimization

If the primal problem were a minimization then we can transform this into an equivalent maximization by multiplying through by −1.

Returning to the problem formulation the canonical primal would be:

$$\text{Max. } 5B + 6.5D$$

subject to:

$$1B + 1D \leq 1200$$
$$3B + 6D \leq 4830$$
$$8B + 4D \leq 5200$$
$$-1B \leq -350$$
$$-1B + -1D \leq -750$$

The dual can now be expressed as a minimization problem consisting of constraints all taking the form $\geq$. The dual becomes:

Minimize $1200U_1 + 4830U_2 + 5200U_3 - 350U_4 - 750U_5$

subject to:

$$1U_1 + 3U_2 + 8U_3 - 1U_4 - 1U_5 \geq 5$$

$$1U_1 + 6U_2 + 4U_3 - 1U_5 \geq 6.5$$

Note that there are five dual variables – one for each constraint in the primal problem – and two constraints – one for each decision variable in the primal problem. The solution to this dual formulation is shown in Table 3.3 below:

Table 3.3   Dual solution: minimization problem

	U_1	U_2	U_3	U_4	U_5	SU_1	SU_2	Value
OF	250	180	0	0	200	350	600	−5650
U_3	0.25	1.5	1	0	−0.25	0	−0.25	1.625
U_4	1	9	0	1	−1	1	−2	8

The OF value in the primal is the same as that in the dual –£5650, which represents the maximum profit given the constraints imposed. The decision variables – B and D – take their value from the corresponding OF row in the dual. Remember that the first 5 variables relate to the constraints in the primal so the last two SU_1 and SU_2 – must relate to the decision variables. Here we have:

$$B = 350$$
$$D = 600$$

as the profit maximizing levels of production. From Property 2 we have:

Constraint 1: slack   = 250
Constraint 2: slack   = 180
Constraint 3: slack   = 0
Constraint 4: surplus = 0
Constraint 5: surplus = 200

So Constraints 3 and 4 are binding at the optimal solution. From the dual we see that:

$$U_3 = 1.625$$
$$U_4 = 8$$

hence these must be the opportunity costs for the two binding constraints.

Sensitivity analysis

We examined sensitivity analysis in its simplest form in Chapter 2 using a graphical method. Such analysis is potentially worthwhile to the manager for two reasons:

- To assess the opportunities for taking managerial action to change the constraints and hence change the current optimal solution. It is all very well knowing what to do in order to maximize profit. But this assumes the manager can do nothing about the constraints faced. This is unrealistic, since a manager will typically have some influence or control over some constraints. More patches could be acquired or more machine time made available. The task of the manager is to determine whether such actions are worthwhile and, if so, their priorities.

- To assess the impact on the solution of uncertainty about the numerical coefficients used in determining the solution. It is unrealistic to assume that the coefficients used in the OF or in the constraints will be 100 per cent accurate or constant. The profit coefficients, for example, are likely to be averages and subject to some variability or even uncertainty. The manager may wish to determine, therefore, the sensitivity of the current optimal solution to changes in such coefficient values.

We shall look at such sensitivity analysis in a number of different ways:

- Changes in the right hand side (RHS) of constraints in maximization problems;
- Changes in the RHS of constraints in minimization problems;
- Changes in the OF for basic variables;
- Changes in the OF for non-basic variables.

Let us return to our basic profit maximization problem and its Simplex solution which we reproduce here (Table 3.4):

Table 3.4   Tableau 4 reiterated

	B	D	S_1	S_2	S_3	Value
OF	0	0	0	−0.8889	−0.292	−5810
S_1	0	0	1	−0.1111	−0.0833	230
D	0	1	0	0.2222	−0.0833	640
B	1	0	0	−0.1111	0.1667	330

We already know from the last section on the dual that the opportunity costs of the two binding constraints are shown in the OF row:

$$S_1 = 0$$
$$S_2 = 0.8889$$
$$S_3 = 0.292$$

The opportunity costs are interpreted in the usual way. They represent the cost to the company of not making extra resources available over and above those we currently have. For patches this cost is zero – we have spare anyway. For machine time the cost is 88.9 p per min for cutting and 29.2 p per min for sewing time. The implication is clear. By not making additional cutting time available we are 'losing' 88.9 p for each extra minute we do not make available. Other things being equal the manager should try to acquire extra machine time since this has the higher opportunity cost. However, the answer to the question: *how much extra of this resource should we acquire?* is much less obvious. Should we acquire 1 extra minute, or 100 or 1000? The general principle is clear. We should acquire as many extra minutes of cutting time as we can profitably use. What happens as we acquire extra quantities of this particular resource? By making extra supplies available we will be changing the combination of production which is optimal. There may well come a point where extra supplies of cutting time by themselves are of no use. We may have altered production to such an extent that we have run out of some other resource. In other words, we may make extra supplies of cutting time available to such an extent that this constraint becomes non-binding. Remember that the two binding constraints are:

$$3B + 6D = 4830$$
$$8B + 4D = 5200$$

If we add 1 to the RHS of the first constraint we already know (from

Chapter 2) that the new solution will be:

$$B = 329.8888$$
$$D = 640.2222$$

The effect on the variables and constraints will then be as shown in Table 3.5.

Table 3.5   Solution changes

	Current solution	New solution	Change
OF	5810	5810.8889	+0.8889
B	330	329.8888	−0.1111
D	640	640.2222	+0.2222
Constraint 1	970	970.1111	+0.1111
Constraint 2	4830	4831	+1
Constraint 3	5200	5200	0

If we examine Tableau 4 we see that the changes in Table 3.5 are the coefficients shown in column S_2 – which relates to the second constraint, the one we are examining. In fact the coefficients in this column indicate the effect on the current optimal solution of a 1 unit increase in the RHS of this constraint without the need for further calculation. If we increased supplies by 2 mins then, logically, the outcome would be twice the change indicated in the S_2 column. That is:

$$
\begin{aligned}
OF &\quad +1.7778 \\
S_1 &\quad -0.2222 \\
D &\quad +0.4444 \\
B &\quad -0.2222
\end{aligned}
$$

Similarly, if we added 3 units there would be a threefold change and so on. If you examine the last calculations you begin to see what is happening to the solution. As we add more cutting time we are switching resources from B to D. We are making use of the added cutting time but we also need additional patches and sewing time. Clearly this can only happen as long as we are still producing B. There will come a time when, having added more and more cutting time, we will be producing zero B and will not be able to increase D production further. Equally, by adding more cutting time we are gradually making use of more of the available patches – S_1, the number of unused patches is declining. Again, using the same logic, there must come a time when, having added more and more cutting time, there are no more unused patches to allow us to increase production further. So, sooner or later extra supplies of cutting time will not allow us to increase profit further. We need to calculate when this will occur. From the tableau we see that the two critical factors – S_1 and B – are those with negative coefficients in the S_2 column. Current values for S_1 and B are 230 and 300 respectively. These values will decline at the rate of –0.1111 and –0.1111 respectively for each extra minute of cutting time that becomes available. So, if we determine the ratio for S_1:

$$\frac{230}{0.1111} = 2070$$

then the value of 2070 indicates the number of extra minutes of cutting time that we can add before S_1 becomes zero. Consider what this implies. We can add up to 2070 extra minutes of cutting time before the first constraint becomes binding – before we run out of unused patches allowing us to increase production. In terms of this constraint, therefore, the figure of 2070 indicates the maximum possible increase in cutting time. For B we have:

$$\frac{330}{0.1111} = 2970$$

which again represents the maximum possible increase in cutting time in the context of B. We are reducing production of B as we make more cutting time available. By making 2970 minutes available we will have reduced B to zero. Further increases in cutting time will have no further effect on profit. It is evident that the smallest of these ratios – for S_1 – will be the most limiting. We now have an answer to the question: given that it is profitable to make extra cutting time available how much extra time should be made available? The answer is no more than 2070 mins. At this point further increases in machine time *by itself* will not help us increase profit further since we will now be short of patches as well. For the other binding constraint – sewing time – the opportunity cost is 2.92 p per minute. The effect on the current solution of more sewing time will be to:

- Reduce unused patches by 0.0833 per minute added;
- Reduce D by 0.0833;
- Increase B by 0.1667.

The maximum worthwhile increase in relation to each constraint can be determined as:

$$S_1 = \frac{230}{0.0833} = 2760$$

$$D = \frac{640}{0.0833} = 7680$$

Accordingly, the maximum worthwhile increase in sewing time will be 2760 mins. This sensitivity analysis has been carried out on constraints taking the form ≤. As we know we may have other types of constraint.

Constraints taking the form ≥

To illustrate this type of constraint let us modify our problem:

$$\text{Max. } 5B + 6.5D$$

subject to:

$$1B + 1D \leq 1200$$
$$3B + 6D \leq 4830$$
$$8B + 4D \leq 5200$$
$$1B \quad\quad \geq 350$$
$$1D \quad \geq 350$$
$$1B + 1D = 750$$

The Simplex solution is given in Table 3.6.

Table 3.6   Simplex solution with constraints taking the form ≥

	B	D	S_1	S_2	S_3	SU_4	SU_5	A_6	Value
OF	0	0	0	0	0	−1.5	0	−6.5	−4350
S_1	0	0	1	0	0	0	0	−1	450
S_2	0	0	0	1	0	−3	0	−6	1380
S_3	0	0	0	0	1	4	0	−4	800
B	1	0	0	0	0	−1	0	0	350
D	0	1	0	0	0	1	0	1	400
SU_5	0	0	0	0	0	1	1	1	50

We have B = 350 (the minimum required) and D = 400 (50 more than the minimum required) giving a total production of 750 – exactly equal to the joint production required. We have slack in each of the three available resources. The binding constraints are Constraint 4 and Constraint 6 – the only columns with non-zero coefficients in the OF row. Note that given the equality in Constraint 6 this will be associated not with a slack or surplus variable but with an artificial variable. Let us examine Constraint 4, ≥. The corresponding variable is SU_4 – the surplus variable, currently zero. Assume, as with the slack variables earlier, that we wish to examine the effect of a change in the RHS of this constraint of 1 unit. In the context of our problem this would imply that we require B ≥ 351, that is, we require at least 351 units of B to be produced. The sensitivity analysis will now indicate what effect this will have on the current solution. First we note the effect on the OF value, at –1.5. Interpretation for this type of constraint is that the OF value will decrease by £1.50 if we increase the RHS by 1. Clearly, given the other binding constraint insisting that total production is 750, the only way we can increase production of B by 1 unit is to decrease D by one unit, causing a change in profit of –£1.50 (+5–6.5). The other effects will be:

S_1	0
S_2	–3
S_3	4
B	–1
D	1
S_5	1

We already know that B will increase by 1 and D decrease. It is evident that we must reverse the signs of these coefficients in the SU4 column to determine the effect. There will be no change in S_1 – unused patches – since the net effect on production is zero. S_2 – unused cutting time – will increase by 3 mins (3 – 6) whilst that of sewing time, S_3, will decrease by 4 mins (8 – 4). Finally, surplus production of D, SU_5, will fall by 1. In the same way as we did before we can determine the maximum change in the RHS value that can occur. This time (because of the sign reversal) we take ratios of Values to positive coefficients and determine the smallest. We have:

$$S_3 \qquad \frac{800}{4} = 200$$

$$D \qquad \frac{400}{1} = 400$$

$$SU_5 \qquad \frac{50}{1} = 50$$

The maximum possible increase in the RHS of this constraint, therefore, will be 50 units. At that point, D will be 350 (that is, with zero surplus) and we cannot increase production of B further without violating the fifth constraint ($D \geq 350$).

Constraints taking the form =

For this type of constraint we must examine the relevant Artificial variable column in the tableau, A_6. The column has an opportunity cost of -6.5, the same as the profit coefficient for D. Suppose we were to increase the RHS of this constraint by 1. This would imply that we must have an extra unit of production, 751. Other things being equal this will be D since this generates more profit than B. The other coefficients in this column indicate the change in the rest of the problem. The other changes will be:

$$
\begin{array}{ll}
S_1 & -1 \\
S_2 & -6 \\
S_3 & -4 \\
B & 0 \\
D & 1 \\
SU_5 & 1
\end{array}
$$

This can be interpreted as (in the order given above) a reduction in spare patches of 1, in spare cutting time of 6 mins, in spare sewing time of 4 mins, no change in B, an increase of 1 in D and an increase in SU_5 of 1. We proceed as before by finding the smallest of the ratios of Values to negative coefficients.

$$S_1 = \frac{450}{1} = 450$$

$$S_2 = \frac{1380}{6} = 230$$

$$S_3 = \frac{800}{4} = 200$$

giving a maximum change of 200 before the third constraint becomes binding.

Minimization problems

We can follow a similar logic with minimization problems. Rather than repeat everything we have done we can simply summarize the process:

Constraint ≤

- The OF coefficient will be positive and indicate the increase in the OF value;
- The column coefficients indicate the change in the variable values;
- The maximum change is determined from the smallest ratio of Value to negative coefficients.

Constraint ≥

- The OF coefficient will be positive and indicate the increase in the OF value;
- The column coefficients must have their signs reversed to indicate the change in the variable values;
- The maximum change is determined from the smallest ratio of Value to positive coefficients.

Constraints =

- The OF coefficient for the relevant artificial variable will be positive and indicate the increase in the OF value;
- The column indicates the change in the variable values;
- The maximum change is determined from the smallest ratio of Value to positive coefficients.

The objective function

We saw in Chapter 2 how we determine the maximum changes in the OF coefficients which can occur before the current solution point changes. To apply this to the Simplex we shall introduce a different problem. Assume the company is considering producing a third type of jean, denoted as L. This generates a profit of £6 per unit produced, requires 1 patch, 5 mins of cutting time and 6 mins of sewing time. Our problem is then:

$$\text{Max. } 5B + 6.5D + 6L$$

subject to:

$$1B + 1D + 1L \leq 1200$$
$$3B + 6D + 5L \leq 4830$$
$$8B + 4D + 6L \leq 5200$$

and the optimal solution is found to be as in Table 3.7.

Table 3.7   Optimal Simplex solution with an additional product

	B	D	L	S_1	S_2	S_3	Value
OF	0	0	−0.1940	0	−0.8889	−0.2920	−5810
S_1	0	0	−0.0556	1	−0.1111	−0.0833	230
D	0	1	0.6111	0	0.2222	−0.0833	640
B	1	0	0.4442	0	−0.1111	0.1667	330

You will see that – with the addition of the L column – the solution is as before. We shall now examine how sensitive this solution is to the OF coefficients. To do this we must distinguish between basic and non-basic variables.

Basic variables

The two basic variables are B and D. If we examine B we can indulge in some simple arithmetic. We take the OF row and the B row and divide OF by B to give:

Table 3.8   Basic variable B

	B	D	L	S_1	S_2	S_3
OF	0	0	−0.1940	0	−0.8889	−0.2920
B	1	0	0.4444	0	−0.1111	0.1667
Ratio row (OF/B)	0	0	−0.437	0	8	−1.75

If we ignore the zero values we see that we have two negative ratios and one positive. The positive ratio, 8, indicates the maximum increase in the B profit coefficient that can occur before the current optimal solution changes. In other words, profit per unit of B can rise to £13 (5 + 8) without changing the current optimal mix of production. If B's profit per unit were to rise to more than £13 then the current solution would change. The negative ratios indicate the equivalent for a decrease in B's profit contribution. Since there are two we choose the smallest of these, at –0.437, to indicate the maximum change that can occur. B's profit can fall to £4.56 (5-0.44) without a change in the current optimal production mix. The production manager knows, therefore, that as long as B's profit margin remains within the range £4.56 to £13 there is no need to alter the production schedule. For D we have (from Table 3.9) –0.32 and +3.5,

Table 3.9 Basic variable D

	B	D	L	S_1	S_2	S_3
OF	0	0	–0.1940	0	–0.8889	–0.2920
D	0	1	0.6111	0	0.2222	–0.0833
Ratio row (OF/D)	0	0	–0.3175	0	–4	3.50

indicating that as long as D's profit contribution is in the range £6.28 to £10 there will be no change in the production mix required to generate maximum profit.

Non-basic variables

But what of the other variable – L – currently non-basic? Clearly a different sort of question arises here. Since L is non-basic we know that it is not sufficiently profitable per unit. A reduction in the contribution therefore will leave the solution unaffected. But what of an increase? Potentially, L could become so profitable it entered the solution – at the expense of one of the other types of jean. We see from the OF row in Table 3.7 that the L column has a coefficient of –0.194. This indicates the increase in L's profit contribution if it is to enter the solution. If L's profit rose above £6.194 then it would become profitable to produce (at the expense of either B or D).

Summary

We have spent some considerable time examining the Simplex method and the information that can be extracted from it for any type of LP problem. One of the reasons for doing this was that the Simplex method lies at the heart of LP, even when using specialist computer software, since it can deal with any type of LP problem of any size. Whilst the use of such software means that we no longer need to concern ourselves with the mechanics of the arithmetic involved, it does not replace the need for someone to be able to interpret the solution information in a problem context. This is why we have gone into so much detail on how the Simplex information at every iteration can be interpreted and used. No organization using LP to assist in its decision-making would be content with simply receiving the optimal solution to an LP problem. The accompanying Simplex information is at least as valuable to the business

Linear programming and computer software

We have deliberately used small problems so far in the text to show clearly the principles of LP at work. In the real world, organizations will not be faced with two-variable problems comprising a small number of constraints. LP models are likely to involve several hundred variables and several thousand constraints. Such problems must be formulated for, and solved by, computer programs. Some students will already be familiar with one of the more popular LP packages used in education: LINDO.[1] In this chapter we shall see how computer software enables us to solve such LP models in the real world.

Microsoft Excel Solver

Spreadsheets have become the calculating workhorse in many organizations and it is perhaps not surprising that they now include optimization capability. This means that we can formulate complex LP problems and solve them readily using an appropriate spreadsheet. One such is Microsoft Excel which comes with a built-in Solver. A typical Solver template is shown in Figure 4.1. The methodology for using Solver is similar to that of the basic LP approach and we shall illustrate as usual with our basic profit maximizing problem. This has been set up in a simple spreadsheet model, shown in Figure 4.2. The three constraints are shown in Rows 5–7. The available supply relating to each constraint is shown in Column B. The amount of each resource currently used is shown in Column C (set to zero initially). Columns D and E show the constraint coefficients. Cells D3 and D4 will eventually show the optimal solution for the number of the two products to manufacture, currently as zero. At the bottom of the spreadsheet we have details of our objective function, profit. The spreadsheet has been set up to show the profit contribution from each product and for total production. What Figure 4.2 does not show are the

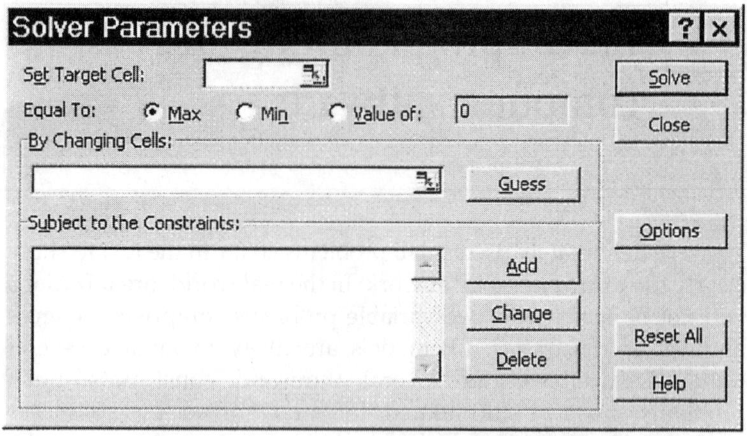

Figure 4.1 Excel Solver template

formulae that must be built into the model for the Solver. These are
shown in Figure 4.3. Cells D11 and E11 contain formulae for their
respective parts of the objective function and D12 shows the total
profit. Cells C5–C7 contain formulae to show the amount of each
resource actually used. The format of the spreadsheet is easily
varied. You could, for example, create two cells containing the
objective function coefficients. These would then be explicitly
visible in the model and Cells D11 and E11 would use the coefficient
cell references in the formulae rather than 5 and 6.5 respectively.

	A	B	C	D	E	F
1						
2				*Basic*	*Design*	
3			Number to make→	0	0	
4	*Constraint*	*Available supply*	*Amount used*			
5	Patches	1200	0	1	1	
6	Cutting	4830	0	3	6	
7	Sewing	5200	0	8	4	
8						
9						
10				*Profit*		
11			By product	£0.00	£0.00	
12			Total	£0.00		
13						
14						

Figure 4.2 Spreadsheet set-up

	A	B	C	D	E	F
1						
2				*Basic*	*Design*	
3			*Number to make→*	0	0	
4	*Constraint*	*Available supply*	*Amount used*			
5	Patches	1200	=$D$3×D5+$E$3×E5	1	1	
6	Cutting	4830	=$D$3×D6+$E$3×E6	3	6	
7	Sewing	5200	=$D$3×D7+$E$3×E7	8	4	
8						
9						
10				*Profit*		
11			*By product*	=5×D3	=6.5×E3	
12			*Total*	+SUM(D11:E11)		
13						
14						

Figure 4.3 Formulae

Having constructed the spreadsheet we can now use the Solver. Figure 4.4 shows the details. The *Target Cell* is set as D12, Total profit. This is the value we are seeking to optimize. *By Changing Cells* is set as D3–E3, the values of the two decision variables, production of B and D. These values are allowed to vary in our search for optimum profit. Finally, the constraints are shown. Because all three of our constraints are in the form ≤, they can be input as a single expression $C5$:$C$7 <= $B$5:$B$7. We could have input each constraint individually instead. Note that the constraints are formulated to state that the Amount Used (which

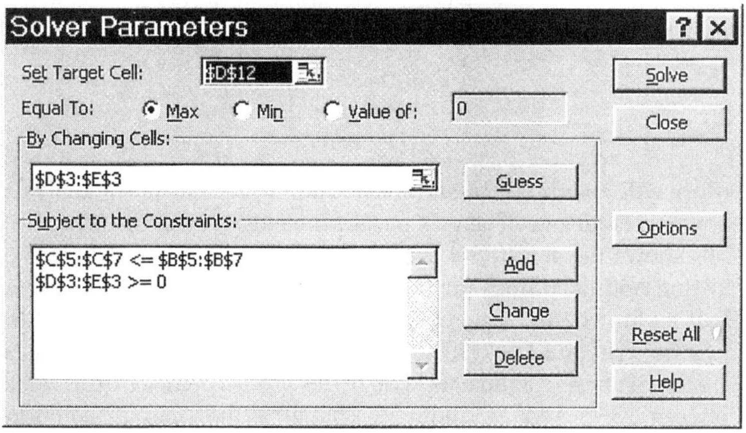

Figure 4.4 Solver details

will be calculated directly from the solution) must be no greater than the available Supply. We have also included the non-negativity constraint. Otherwise, the Solver has no way of knowing that negative values are meaningless in the problem context. Note also that the *Equal To* button has been set to Max since we have a maximization problem. Clicking on the Solve button then transforms the spreadsheet into that shown in Figure 4.5. The cells containing formulae (all previously zero) have now been calculated

	A	B	C	D	E	F
1						
2				*Basic*	*Design*	
3			*Number to make→*	330	640	
4	*Constraint*	*Available supply*	*Amount used*			
5	Patches	1200	970	1	1	
6	Cutting	4830	4830	3	6	
7	Sewing	5200	5200	8	4	
8						
9						
10				*Profit*		
11			*By product*	£1,650.00	£4,160.00	
12			*Total*	£5,810.00		
13						
14						

Figure 4.5 Solution

to show their value at the optimal solution and the optimal values for the two decision variables shown in cells D3 and E3. The solution is the one that we derived both graphically in Chapter 2 and with the Simplex in Chapter 3:

$$\text{Profit} = \pounds 5810$$
$$B = 300$$
$$D = 640$$

Solver will also produce summary output for sensitivity analysis shown in Figure 4.6. The first part of the output labelled *Adjustable Cells* shows the sensitivity analysis on the objective function. The existing optimal values for the decision variables are shown (D9–D10) as are the existing objective function coefficients (F9–F10). Cells G9–G10 and H9–H10 show the maximum allowable changes to each of these coefficients. For B the profit coefficient can vary between £3.25 and £13 without changing the optimal solution whilst for D the range is £2.5 to £10.

	A	B	C	D	E	F	G	H
1		Microsoft Excel 8.0a Sensitivity Report						
2		Worksheet: [prob1.xls]Sheet1						
3		Report created: 08/07/00 13:36:45						
4								
5								
6	Adjustable Cells							
7				Final	Reduced	Objective	Allowable	Allowable
8		Cell	Name	Value	Cost	Coefficient	Increase	Decrease
9		$D$3	Number to make→Basic	330	0	5	8	1.75
10		$E$3	Number to make→Design	640	0	6.5	3.5	4
11								
12	Constraints							
13				Final	Shadow	Constraint	Allowable	Allowable
14		Cell	Name	Value	Price	R.H. Side	Increase	Decrease
15		$C$5	Patches Amount Used	970	0	1200	1E+30	230
16		$C$6	Cutting Amount Used	4830	0.8889	4830	2070	2880
17		$C$7	Sewing Amount Used	5200	0.2917	5200	2760	1980

Figure 4.6 Sensitivity analysis

The second part of the output labelled *Constraints* shows the sensitivity analysis on each of the constraints. The current amount of each constraint required is shown in D15–D17. The Shadow Price (or opportunity cost) is shown in E15–E17. Columns G and H show the maximum increases and decreases allowed in each constraint. In our sensitivity analysis in Chapter 3 we only calculated the increases in constraint values.

Given the amount of analysis that is undertaken on spreadsheets today, the ability to solve LP problems with them is a major advance. However, formulating and solving large, complex problems can be quite awkward and care must be taken with many of the options available in the spreadsheet (such as number of decimal places shown in results).

XPRESS-MP[2]

Given the importance of LP for business decision-making it is not surprising that purpose-written software has become available. Until relatively recently, specialist LP software was typically purpose-built using high level languages and frequently written for one specific task or project. They were rarely user-friendly and difficult to update and alter to changing problem circumstances.

XPRESS-MP is fairly typical of the software that is now available and it is the availability of generic, user-friendly software that has contributed to the popularity of LP as a business modelling approach.

In fact, XPRESS-MP provides a family of inter-related modelling and optimizing software. The two basic components are the *model builder* and the *optimizer*. The model builder component allows the user to build an LP model, reads in the data to be used and creates a standard format for the problem that can then be solved using the optimizer. The model builder is also used to interpret the solution found by the optimizer and export the solution to other packages such as a word processing or graphics package.

Problems are constructed in the model builder using a fairly simple algebraic modelling language that allows for standardization. The model builder for our standard 2 variable, 3 constraint LP problem is shown in Figure 4.7. We first define the decision variables in the model as *b* and *d*. Notice that we can insert comments into the model builder by prefacing with the character ! Such comments assist in the documentation and explanation of the model to other users and perhaps to ourselves the next time we use

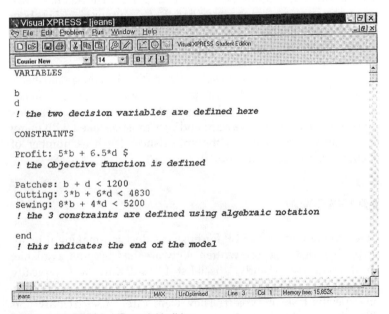

Figure 4.7 XPRESS–MP model builder

it. We then define the constraints of the model, including the objective function using standard algebraic notation. Each constraint must be named first and then defined. The objective function is identified in the model using the $ symbol at the end of the definition. One quirk of the XPRESS-MP system is that constraint inequalities appear as follows:

< indicates a ≤ constraint
> indicates a ≥ constraint

Note that, unlike Solver, we do not need to specify non-negativity constraints. These are assumed automatically in XPRESS-MP. Once the model has been built we can then move to the optimizer. For LP problems the optimizer uses the Simplex approach and the optimizer dialogue box is shown in Figure 4.8. This confirms that the solution method will be the Simplex. At this stage we must also set the direction of the objective function (Max or Min) since this is not actually specified in the model builder. We do this by setting the *Sense* to the MAX direction. The model is then ready to be solved and the Results dialogue box is shown in Figure 4.9 together with the solution. More detailed sensitivity analysis is also available on both constraints and the objective function.

With our small problem the usefulness of such a specialist package is not immediately apparent but a number of comments are worth making. The model builder facility offers a number of advantages. The first is that, in the real world where LP problems can comprise several hundred decision variables and several

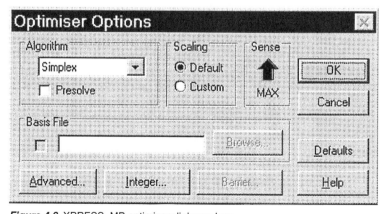

Figure 4.8 XPRESS–MP optimizer dialogue box

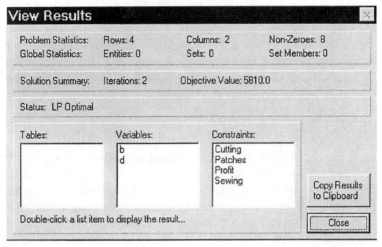

Figure 4.9 Results dialogue box

thousand constraints, the correct formulation of the LP problem to
be solved is the most difficult, and frustrating, part of the exercise.
LP problem formulations typically evolve over a period of time
often on a trial-and-error basis. A powerful, yet simple, model
builder is invaluable in this. Secondly, even when the LP model has
been designed there is likely to be some experimentation with the
model once the initial optimum solution has been analysed.
Managers will typically wish to change some of the key model
parameters and assumptions to help them see what would happen
to the optimum solution and thus help their decision-making.
Again, the model builder supports this approach. Finally, the
person building the LP model and the person using the solution
results are not always the same people. LP modelling requires
considerable expertise and will frequently be done by a specialist.
The user of the model, however, may well be a production manager,
a logistics manager, an accountant with limited knowledge of – or
interest in – LP. However, because the model builder can interface
with other packages – like spreadsheets, graphics and word
processing – that the user will be more familiar with, the results of
the model will be of value to the user even if the rest of the solution
process is very 'black-box'.

A second useful aspect of the software that is not immediately
apparent is that the optimizer will examine the model for errors and
inconsistencies before a solution is attempted. Again, with large,

complex models this feature should not be underestimated. A large amount of time will be spent at the LP formulation stage trying to ensure an accurate formulation of the business problem. No matter how much effort is put into this, with large complex formulations errors and inconsistencies will creep in. Redundant constraints may appear, infeasible problems may be developed and so on. The use of a modelling programme allows these to be noted and tracked and the model debugged, as Figure 4.10 illustrates.

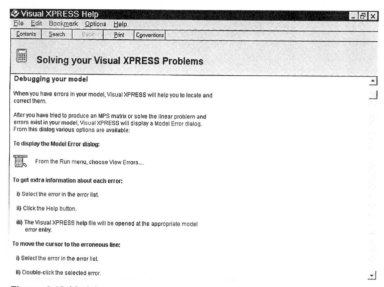

Figure 4.10 Model errors

Summary

There can be little doubt that the developments in LP parallel those in computer hardware and processing power and that the availability of cheap, powerful and user-friendly software has done much to expand the use of LP in business and industry. As Orden (1993) comments, in 1947 before the availability of computers the solution of a 9-constraint problem took 120 person hours of work. From 1950 it was reasonable to solve problems via computer with up to 200 constraints. By 1960 this had increased to 1000 constraints, by 1970 to 10 000 constraints, by 1980 up to 100 000 constraints and by 1990 up to a million constraints. At the same time, however, the development of spreadsheet and specialist software implies an ever

important need for an adequate understanding of the principles –
and limitations – of the LP model if such models are to be used
effectively to assist the decision-maker.

Notes

1. LINDO (www.lindo.com), Microsoft, Excel Solver (www.microsft.com) and
   XPRESS-MP (www.dash.co.uk) are all copyright trademarks.

2. I am grateful to Dash Associates for permission to reproduce the material from
   XPRESS-MP.

5 | LP in the real world

In this chapter we discuss a number of applications of LP to real-world problems. We examine the application itself, the development of an appropriate LP model, the outcomes of the application and we discuss some of the wider issues arising from the application.

Santos seaport, Brazil

This application is based on the article 'Keep the coffee coming' by D. Reis, *OR Insight*, 4:3 (1991), pp. 7–9.

Santos is the main seaport in Brazil with a capacity for handling around 50 ships at any one time. The management of activities at a busy port like Santos are a complex business, particularly the loading and unloading of cargo for ships that have arrived or that are leaving. Such port operations are very labour intensive and require careful planning and coordination with the types of ships in port, their cargoes and the destinations of these cargoes. The cargoes carried by ships can vary widely from agricultural produce such as coffee and cereals, to refrigerated fruit, to frozen meat, to containers. Similarly the type of activity or operation required can vary: loading, unloading, transferring cargo from ships to warehouses on the port site, so-called complementary services dealing with routine cleaning and mail-handling. The labour-force planning has to try to match the work required by the ships in port with the skills and experience of the available staff and link both of these to available equipment like cranes and fork lift trucks. Sending a highly-trained (and expensive) crane operator to do routine cleaning on a newly arrived ship is hardly likely to be the best use of resources.

The company responsible for operating the port facility were interested in seeing whether it was possible to develop a model for labour planning in order to improve labour productivity and the productivity of equipment and facilities (given these will often have high capital costs associated with them). Ultimately, the company's

concern was to try to minimize labour costs yet at the same time
ensure they had the right people doing the right job at the right time
with the right equipment.

It was decided to develop an LP model for a planning period of
a month. The objective was to minimize total monthly labour costs.
The model constraints were formulated in terms of the availability
of labour, the total tonnage of cargo to be handled at each type of
operation and minimum requirements for certain categories of
labour to certain types of operations. The final model resulted in
some 400 variables and 100 constraints. As is usual with LP model
development it was necessary to develop a simplified set of
variables and constraints given the complexity of the port
operations. Eleven different categories of labour were identified
and these became the model's decision variables:

> Cargo annotators
> Chauffeurs
> Equipment operators (such as cranes)
> Foremen
> Operations staff
> Ship agents
> Staff involved in loading and unloading
> Staff involved in loading/unloading specifically in warehouse
>   and ships
> Staff supervising engineering personnel
> Truck drivers
> Warehouse storekeepers.

The model, like most in LP, required considerable data including:

- Total tonnage to be handled for each type of operation.
- Degree of specialization of the incoming ships.
- Indices of productivity for each category of labour and for
  equipment.
- Hourly wage costs for each category of labour.
- Hourly costs for each type of equipment.
- Expected availability of labour hours and equipment hours.

Some of this data was already available within the organization.
However, there were considerable data gaps which required new
data collection procedures. One of the initial difficulties to
overcome was persuading those staff involved that this was an
important task (at the beginning there was a view that there were

more important things to do than gather data for someone else). This was achieved by company staff and the modelling consultants explaining the purpose of the project and the need for the additional data.

The model was effectively trying to answer the question: what amounts of the different categories of labour (and equipment through the constraints) should be allocated to the different types of operation/activity in order to minimize total costs? The outputs from the model included:

* The labour requirements across the 11 defined categories.
* The requirements for the various types of equipment.
* The schedule of operations for handling cargo.
* Forecasts of additional labour hours required to handle demand peaks.

In addition to the monetary savings generated – estimated at several hundred thousand dollars a year in reduced labour costs – the model has also allowed the company to undertake a variety of 'what-if' analyses. Again, this is a common situation in real-world LP. Management are often more interested in undertaking sensitivity analysis than in the optimal solution itself. Three different scenarios of varying assumptions considered to be optimistic, most likely and pessimistic were developed to allow management to assess alternative futures for the business. Management can also use the model to assess the impact and cost-effectiveness of introducing new equipment and to assess the impact of random events such as severe weather.

Brunswick Smelting, Canada

This application is based on the article 'Led by LP!' by G. Warren, J. Bhadury and J. Hemenway, *OR Insight*, 7:3 (1994) pp. 12–21.

Brunswick Mine and Smelting (BMS) is a lead smelter based in New Brunswick, Canada and is composed of three profit-centre divisions: a mine, a smelter and a fertilizer plant. The smelting division produces lead by using a raw material known as lead feed. The lead feed is purchased from different sources, including other divisions within the company, and the chemical composition varies from source to source although it remains relatively consistent within any one source. The feed from different sources is mixed together and used to produce a variety of lead products. The company routinely had to decide on the best mix of inputs (lead feeds) from the available sources and the best mix of outputs (lead products).

At the time the model was developed, the company, like many of its competitors in North America, was facing considerable challenges. The number of sources for purchasing lead feed was on the increase but with considerably variations in quality and price. Demand for lead products was decreasing (for example. because of the removal of lead from petrol fuels) with a trend towards orders for more specialist products in smaller quantities. Prices of lead products had, as a consequence of falling demand, reduced with obvious consequences for company profitability and for increased competition. At the same time, overseas competition was increasing with such competitors having the advantage of lower labour costs. All in all, this had created a very turbulent but uncertain operating environment and had considerably complicated the process of deciding on the best feed and product mix.

The modelling team reviewed the whole production process and, after discussion with company management, formulated the problem as an LP problem. The objective was to maximize the profit margin between the product revenue and the feed cost. This would determine the optimal mix of feeds (which are constrained by both cost and blending requirements) and products (which are based on the specific lead feeds used, revenues and the technical efficiency of the production process). There were a total of 11 feed sources available (some internal and some external) and seven key products (such as refined lead, lead bismuth alloy). Product revenues and feed costs were both positive and negative for the mix of variables used. For two of the feeds the company was actually paid by the supplier to use them (hence increasing the use of these feeds will, other things being equal, actually increase revenue rather than costs). One of the products, furnace slag, was actually a by-product of the production process rather than a marketable product. Its revenue was therefore negative: the company incurred a cost for getting rid of it.

As with most LP models, certain key assumptions had to be made in order to keep the model manageable. Amongst these were that: product and lead feed prices would remain unchanged over the planning period; that the chemical composition of both products and lead feeds remain constant over time; that supplies of lead feeds are available on demand and that there are no carry-overs of supplies or products between periods. Whilst all of these assumptions could be accommodated by further developing the LP model they would add further complications and complexities both to the model formulation and to the interpretation of the solution.

The constraints used fell into four categories:

- Feed blending: these related to the requirements of the chemical composition of the feed and typically comprised minimum and/or maximum composition requirements.
- Feed availability: these related to maximum supply availability of the different sources of feed. Interestingly, it proved difficult to predict exact availability of supplies so estimates were required instead.
- Production.
- Conservation: constraints requiring metals to the smelter are equal to the mass of metals in the products.

Three types of decision variables were used (45 variables in total) relating to feed, product and internal. Feed and product variables related to the tonnage of each variable that would be used. The internal variables were used in order to generate operational information that would be used by management to monitor operations (for example the total amount of lead in the plant at any one time). An optimal solution was determined (the team used LINDO for the solution process) showing the maximum profit margin that was attainable (around $50m) together with the optimal feed and product mix quantities.

Although the model generated an optimal solution, management was actually more interested in the sensitivity analysis that could then be conducted (which in part was completed on a spreadsheet). Amongst the findings from this analysis were:

- The optimal solution was effectively price-insensitive. That is, the solution was relatively unaffected by changes in feed and product prices.
- One of the sources of feed supply currently used was a nearby mine owned by the parent company. In the optimal solution this supply did not appear in the solution (that is, was not actually required). This instigated a further financial evaluation of the effects of not using this supply.

- Two of the composition constraints were particularly binding and further analysis was undertaken into the effects of relaxing these requirements on the final product quality.
- The need for better estimates for some of the data parameters used in the model.

It also became apparent that two further developments should be investigated. The first was to consider integrating the LP model into a decision support system that would enable management to assess optimal decisions online. The second related to the development of a group-wide information systems given the trading connections between many individual companies within the group.

Aluminium recycling

This application is based on the article 'Exploiting the scraps' by M. Hasan and I. Osman, *OR Insight*, 9:3 (1996), pp. 13–8.

The Arabian Light Metals Company (ALMC) is the largest manufacturer of aluminium profiles (bars) in Kuwait supplying just over one third of the local market demand. Its product is used by local industry to produce aluminium doors, windows and sheeting for kitchens and bathrooms. The profiles are produced to Kuwaiti government standards. The profiles are themselves made from aluminium billets (cylinder bars) which are either imported or made in-house by ALMC. The in-house production of billets is made of a combination of pure metals and aluminium scrap which comes either from ALMC's own production or is bought from the local scrap metal market.

Over the last few years the cost of imported billets has nearly doubled and ALMC is looking to produce low-cost billets to increase profitability, preferably by utilizing more of the local scrap in its production since this can be bought relatively cheaply. The problem, however, is that the profiles must be manufactured to tightly defined guidelines in term of the mix of the various metals used with minimum and maximum percentages for nine of the different metal ingredients.

The overall aim of the LP model, then, was to try to determine the optimal mix of the different types of aluminium scrap and pure metals that would minimize production cost whilst meeting the required product quality standards.

The model was formulated to involve:

- A set of decision variables defining the quantities of scrap and pure metals.
- A set of constraints reflecting the quality/mix requirements.
- A set of constraints for the available quantities of each type of scrap.
- A constraint relating to the capacity of the furnace used in the production process.
- An objective function.

The notation used for the model is fairly typical of that developed for many real-world LP models. Whilst it looks particularly complex we show part of it here to illustrate the approach. Typically, LP models make use of what is known as subscript notation when dealing with, as here, multiple inputs and outputs. For example, suppose we have four scrap types X_1, X_2, X_3, X_4 which we measure in tons. Each of these will have a cost C_1, C_2, C_3, C_4. We could then write our objective function as:

$$\text{Min. } C_1X_1 + C_2X_2 + C_3X_3 + C_4X_4$$

Similarly since one of the constraints relates to the capacity of the furnace we could write:

$$X_1 + X_2 + X_3 + X_4 \leq F$$

where F is the capacity (in tons) of the furnace.

For large problems with many decision variables this notation gets cumbersome and awkward. Subscript notation allows a much more concise formulation (but does need a little getting used to). In our example we would use a subscript i where i could take a value from 1 to 4:

$$i = 1...4$$

we could then show the objective function as:

$$\Sigma C_i X_i$$

where Σ is a symbol simply indicating that we sum (or add together) each of the values as i takes successive values from 1 to 4. Similarly our furnace constraint would become:

$$\Sigma X_i \leq F$$

For ALMC the model builders used the following notation:

i = an index for the type of scrap ($i = 1,...,k$)

l = an index for the type of pure material ($l = k+1,...,n$)

a_{il} = the percentage of the lth pure metal in the ith scrap

C_i = the cost of the ith scrap/material type

F = the capacity of the furnace

S_i = the available quantity of the ith scrap type

L_l = the lower percentage limits of the lth pure material required to meet the defined quality standard

U_l = the upper percentage limits of the lth pure material required to meet the defined quality standard

X_i = the decision variables, the amounts of the scrap types and pure materials to use.

The formulation was developed as:

Min. $\Sigma C_i X_i$ The cost of the scrap types and pure materials used

s.t.

$\Sigma X_i \leq F$ The furnace constraint

$\Sigma a_{il} X_i \leq U_l F$ Upper limit quality constraints

$\Sigma a_{il} X_i \geq L_l F$ Lower limit constraints

$X_i \leq S_i$ Supply constraints

$\Sigma a_{im} X_i > R$ A chemical constraint requiring the ratio between the contents of

$\Sigma a_{is} X_i$ Magnesium (m) and silicon (s) to be greater than a given constant R.

The optimal solution from the model provided management with the details of the various quantities of scrap and pure materials required for production. The optimal solution resulted in a reduced production cost with a saving of some US$6000 for each day's production. In addition, the solution enabled ALMC to recycle all of its own scrap and produce a final product that actually exceeded the quality requirements. Analysis also revealed an opportunity to reduce costs further by introducing a third production shift each day (existing production was centred around two 8-hour shifts per day).

Summary

LP is not simply an academic subject. It is a practical tool to help decision-makers in many business organizations. However, the practicalities of developing and applying an LP model to a business problem are typically complex and expertise, experience and determination are all required, particularly when developing an LP model in an organization which has not used them before. The case studies summarized in this chapter reveal a number of issues common to many LP developments. These include:

- *LP is a 'data hungry' technique.*
  The larger and more complex the model becomes then the more data it requires both in terms of constraint relationships and of numerical parameters. For many organizations obtaining accurate and up-to-date data can be a challenge in itself. In many cases, as illustrated with these examples, the data required by the model may not currently be collected or be available requiring additional data collection costs and, perhaps, delaying the development and use of the model.

- *LP is only a model.*
  LP formulates a model of the business problem. Like any model this will only be an approximation of reality. For a variety of reasons – lack of data, the need for simplification – the model will have some number of assumptions built into it. These assumptions will be critical to the reliability, accuracy and usefulness of the solution produced. Sensitivity analysis can play a useful part at identifying the impact of changing certain key assumptions.

- *LP requires trial and error.*
  In the real world an LP model will not be perfected at the first iteration. Trial-and-error development will take place both on the formulation and the solution, assessing the effect of different assumptions and of different ways of representing constraints.

- *Involving the decision-maker.*
  LP is a complex and sophisticated technique requiring considerable expertise. However, it is unlikely that the LP practitioner will also be the business decision-maker and that, equally, the decision-maker will be an LP expert. The more successful LP applications have ensured a partnership between

the two, involving the decision-maker in the project from the beginning, using their knowledge of the business to test the assumptions, constraints and elements of the model and also using their knowledge to check that the mathematical solution makes sense in a business context.

6 | LP: Where next?

Linear programming has come a long way since the development of the simplex method just over 50 years ago. In this chapter we shall review some of the major developments that have taken place in, and around, LP and consider where future developments may take the technique.

Specialist LP applications

As the application literature around LP has built up, a number of specialist areas of LP have developed. Effectively, these are groupings of LP applications applied to common problems. Such groupings have led to the development of specialist solution algorithms and an extensive library of applications, enabling LP practitioners to take short cuts in problem formulation by looking at other similar formulations. Amongst the most common groupings are the following.

Resource allocation/product mix problems

In fact, the problem we have used throughout this text falls into this category. Such problems are typically concerned with optimizing the allocation of scarce resources and/or optimizing the mix of production of some products.

Production scheduling

Production scheduling is often an extension of the resource allocation/product mix problem. Typically for many organizations optimal solutions will be required for a number of consecutive time periods. The jeans problem, for example, will require a solution not just for one day's production but for a sequence of days, perhaps over the next calendar month. Production scheduling problems are typically concerned with this type of scenario where additional factors such as stock control or inventory policies will also have an impact.

Labour scheduling

A similar scheduling approach is often required with problems relating to labour requirements and labour availability. A hospital, for example, might operate a shift system for its nursing staff consisting of three 8-hour shifts during each 24-hour period. It will have a known number of nursing staff available with different skills and qualifications and will face different levels of demand for such staff between shifts, between different days and possibly between different parts of the year.

Blending/diet/feed-mix problems

These problems revolve around a requirement to mix together some set of ingredients or raw materials in such a way that the mix must meet certain specified criteria. Applications range from the food industry to the chemical industry to the oil industry.

Marketing and media applications

Media applications typically involve the search for an optimal mix of advertising (TV, radio, Internet and so on) subject to various constraints relating to costs and advertising effectiveness. Marketing problems typically involve the search for an optimal allocation of marketing time and effort in order to generate additional sales.

Financial problems

Financial problems often involve the search for some optimal investment portfolio where maximum financial return is required subject to constraints relating to portfolio mix, attitudes to risk and varying rates of return. Other common financial problems relate to the area of capital budgeting where a fixed capital budget has to be allocated between competing projects.

Trimloss/cutting stock problems

These problems are essentially concerned with minimizing wastage in any process which requires cutting material from a given supply size. Applications have included the clothing industry, paper-making and glassmaking.

Development of other MP models

Although LP was the first mathematical programming model to be developed, others have followed in fairly rapid succession. Some of these have developed to overcome some of the restrictions/ assumptions inherent in LP, others have developed to focus on specialist areas of optimization.

Integer programming

LP assumes that decision variables are continuous – they can take any numerical value within the constraints set. In our jeans problem this implies that we might have generated a solution where we were to produce 300.6 pairs of jeans, for example, which would clearly be nonsensical. In many LP applications, this may not cause management any great problems. In other cases, however, we may wish to ensure that our model only generates integer solutions for the decision variables. For example, we may have a problem which, in part, requires a decision on how many new factories to construct to meet anticipated demand for our products. Clearly, a non-integer solution is meaningless here. Whilst this could be incorporated into many LP formulations, the approach required is often quite clumsy. Unsurprisingly, integer linear programming (ILP) has developed as an approach in its own right. Integer programming problems will fall into the category of either all integer LP – where all the decision variables are required to be integer – or a mixed integer LP (MILP) – where some of the decision variables are required to be integer whilst the remainder are continuous. It is important to be aware that ILP uses a different solution approach – there are a number of different approaches available – to LP with a more complex algorithm because of the additional integer requirements.

Goal programming

LP requires a single objective function. There will be decision situations where multiple objectives may be appropriate (and where occasionally these differing objectives may conflict with each other). In such a case goal programming may be an appropriate optimization approach since it was developed specifically to deal with multiple objective decision problems. In the jeans example, as an illustration, we may develop multiple objectives which relate to profit maximization but also to maximizing customer satisfaction and minimizing additional investment. Again, the formulation of goal programming problems and their solution differs from those of LP.

Non-linear programming

It is easy to forget that, by definition, LP is appropriate only for these decision situations where linear relationships apply. Clearly, this will not always be the case. There will be occasions where the objective function and/or some of the constraints take a non-linear form. Whilst in principle any type of non-linear relationship may exist, only certain types of non-linear problems can realistically be solved and, again, alternative solution methods have been developed for specific categories of non-linear problems. Because of this it is perhaps not surprising that LP practitioners will often seek to develop linear approximations of non-linear relationships in order to be able to apply LP to some problem.

Data envelopment analysis (DEA)

The development of DEA models and their application has seen a considerable growth over the last decade or so. DEA uses an LP approach to assess the relative efficiency of a group of decision-making units (DMU's), typically within one organization. DMU's might include bank branches, retail outlets, hospitals, schools, area offices. Not surprisingly, given some of the wider economic changes that have taken place (with trends towards downsizing and outsourcing in both public and private sectors), DEA has attracted considerable interest amongst decision-makers. DEA effectively uses LP to measure the outputs achieved by different DMU's from the inputs provided. Outputs might include profitability, sales, number of patients treated, exam passes. Inputs might include finance, staff, equipment, facilities. At the end of the analysis DEA is able to identify those DMU's which are relatively efficient at converting inputs into outputs and those which are relatively inefficient. Potentially, this gives management extremely valuable information on the relative performance of the DMU's within the organization.

Algorithm development

As we have seen, LP applications comprising several thousand decision variables and constraints are not uncommon and are readily solved using the computer technology and software that is now readily available. In the early stages of LP development, however, considerable time and effort was devoted to developing and refining the solution algorithms used to solve LP problems. This development, of course, took place in parallel with the development of large mainframe computers available to government and industry. Even today, however, solution algorithms are constantly reviewed and refined and the LP literature routinely reports such developments. A number of developments are worthy of note.

The first of these is the *interior point* method of solution. As we know, the Simplex method is an algorithm which searches for an optimal solution by moving from one corner point (or vertex) of the feasible area (which can be viewed as a polyhedron) to another by moving along the edge of the polyhedron. Interior point methods take a different approach and for certain type of LP problems such methods can offer considerable savings in solution times. Interior point methods start from a position *within* the feasible area and not from a vertex (corner point) of the feasible area as does the Simplex. The methods then develop towards an optimal solution by moving through the interior of the feasible area but without touching the boundary of the feasible area. The end result of an interior points method LP solution is *approximately* optimal, unlike the Simplex which provides an optimal solution.

The second area of considerable development links to that of interior point methods: the development of so-called *hybrid algorithms*. For certain types of large LP problems such algorithms appear to offer considerable benefit in terms of solution efficiency. Typically such algorithms use interior point methods to find a *nearly* optimal solution. The second step is to use so-called purification procedures to find a basic solution. The third stage is to use this basic solution as the initial solution for the Simplex algorithm which can then iterate to the optimal solution.

Two other areas of development are those of *warm starts* and of *crashing*. A warm start is effectively a solution which forms an initial starting point for the solution algorithm. Such a solution may have been generated from an earlier solution of the problem or may be a good guess as to a likely solution (packages such as XPRESS-MP allow for such things). They can provide considerable benefits in terms of solution efficiency and solution speeds. A crash basis results when we force certain variables into the solution at the beginning rather than wait for them to be introduced iteratively. We may choose to do this because we know that certain decision variables will be in the optimal solution. Again, given the number of iterations that the Simplex has to complete in a large problem this can considerably speed up solutions.

Modelling and reporting developments

As discussed already in Chapter 4, the development of modelling and reporting software in LP has contributed significantly to its resurgence and ever-widening application, and it is likely that further significant developments will take place in this area. Modelling developments are likely to include both improved algebraic modellers (along the lines of LINDO and XPRESS-MP) and visual modelling. The former will include even more enhanced interfaces with spreadsheets and databases providing a more integrated approach for decision-makers. The latter would enable a visual model to be developed (of a production process in a factory, for example) and then a mathematical expression linking parts of the visual model could be introduced: the capacity of the production line, for example, or the time taken to replenish stocks. The LP solution could then be visibly linked to the visual model with considerable benefit to the non-specialist's understanding and use of the results.

Conclusion

There is no doubt that LP has made immense progress over the last 50 years in terms both of solution methods and areas of application. It is equally likely that the next 50 years will see further developments, particularly in extending the areas to which LP can be applied and the number of decision-makers who use it as a routine tool.

Bibliography

Antunes, A.P. (1999). 'Location analysis helps manage solid waste in Portugal', *Interfaces*, 29 pp. 32–43.

Avramovich, D., Cook, T.M., Langston, G.D. and Sutherland, F. (1982). 'A decision support system for fleet management: a linear programming approach', *Interfaces*, 12, pp.1–9.

Arntzen, B.C., Brown, G.C., Harrison, T.P. and Trafton, L.L. (1995). 'Global Supply Management at Digital Equipment Corporation', *Interfaces*, 25, pp. 69–93.

Ashford, R.W. and Daniel, R.C. (1991). 'Practical aspects of mathematical programming'. In A.G. Munford and T.C. Bailey (eds), *Operational Research Tutorial Papers*. Birmingham: Operational Research Society.

Baker, B.M. (1993). 'Bags you choose – optimising blood pack usage in a regional transfusion centre', *OR Insight*, 6: 3, pp. 3–7.

Bodington, C.E. and Baker, T.E. (1990). 'A history of mathematical programming in the petroleum industry', *Interfaces*, 20, pp. 117–27.

Bouzaher, A. and Offutt, S. (1992). 'A stochastic linear programming model for corn residue production'. *Journal of the Operational Research Society*, 43, pp. 843–57.

Chen, M. and Wang, W. (1998). 'A linear programming model for integrated steel production and distribution planning', *International Journal of Operations and Production Management*, 17: 6, pp. 592–610.

Clark, D.N. and Finlay, P.N. (1990). 'Chartwell Books: a case study in mathematical modelling', *Journal of the Operational Research Society*, 41, pp. 1095–1109.

Dantzig, G.B. (1951). 'Application of the simplex method to a transportation problem'. In T.C. Koopmans (ed.), *Activity Analysis of Production and Allocation*, pp. 359–73. New York: Wiley.

Dantzig, G.B. (1963). *Linear Programming and Extensions*. Princeton, NJ: Princeton University Press.

De Angelis, V. (1998). 'Planning home assistance for AIDS patients in the city of Rome, Italy', *Interfaces*, 28 pp. 75–83.

Dillon, J.E. and Kontogiorgis, S. (1999). 'US Airways optimizes the scheduling of reserve flight crews', *Interfaces*, 29, pp. 123–31.

Duffuaa, S.O., Al-Zayer, J.A. Al-Marhoun, M.A. and Al-Sayeh, M.A. (1992). 'A linear programming model to evaluate gas availability for vital industries in Saudi Arabia'. *Journal of the Operational Research Society*, 43, pp. 1035–45.

Dyson, R.G. and Gregory, A.S. (1974). 'The cutting stock problem in the glass industry', *Operational Research Quarterly*, 25, pp. 41-54.

El-Geriani, A.M., Essamin, O. and Loucks, D.P. (1998). 'Water from the desert: minimising costs of meeting Libya's water demands'. *Interfaces*, 28, pp. 23-35.

Farley, A.A. (1991). 'Planning the cutting of photographic color paper rolls for Kodak (Australasia) Pty Ltd.', *Interfaces*, 21, pp. 96–106.

Gilmore, P.C. and Gomory, R.E. (1961). 'A linear programming approach to the cutting stock problem', *Operations Research*, 9, 849–59.

Greenberg, H.J. (1993). 'How to analyse the results of linear programs, Part 1: Preliminaries', *Interfaces*, 23, pp. 56-67.

Greenberg, H.J. (1993). 'How to analyse the results of linear programs, Part 2: Price interpretation', *Interfaces*, 23, pp. 97–114.

Greenberg, H.J. (1993). 'How to analyse the results of linear programs, Part 3: Infeasibility', *Interfaces*, 23, pp. 120–39.

Greenberg, H.J. (1994). 'How to analyse the results of linear programs, Part 4: Forcing substructures', *Interfaces*, 24, pp. 21-130.

Huang, G.H. Baetz, B.W. and Patry, C.G. (1998). 'Trash flow allocation: planning under uncertainty' *Interfaces*, 28, pp. 36–55.

Jacques, A. Eldridge, D. Danielson, P. and Brown, S. (1993). 'Getting the mix right: plant scheduling and marketing optimisation at Shell Chemicals using a linear program based visually interactive scheduling system'. *OR Insight*, 6:1, pp. 15–19.

Olshansky, M. and Gal, S. (1990). 'Optimizing the supply of water: a linear programming approach helps to save pumping costs', *OR Insight*, 3:2, pp. 17–20.

Orden, A. (1993). 'LP from the '40s to the '90s', *Interfaces*, 23, pp. 2–12.

Ormerod, R. (1997). 'OR models assist the Sizewell B public enquiry: the NCB's use of linear programming'. *OR Insight*, 10:3, pp. 2–7.

Subramanian, R., Scheff, R.P., Quinlan, J.D., Wiper, D.S. and Marsten, R.E. (1994). Coldstart: Fleet assignment at Delta Air Lines. *Interfaces*, 24, pp. 104–120.

Williams, H.P. and Redwood, A.C. (1973). 'A structured linear programming model in the food industry', *Operational Research Quarterly*, 25, pp. 517–28.

Wisniewski, M. and Dacre, T. (1990). *Mathematical Programming: Optimization models for Business and Management*. London: McGraw Hill.

Other mathematical programming

Arbel, A. (1994). *Exploring Interior-Point Linear Programming Algorithms and Software*. London: MIT Press.

Ashford, R.W. and Daniel, R.C. (1992). 'Some lessons in solving practical integer programming problems'. *Journal of the Operational Research Society*, 43, pp. 425–33.

Bazaraa, M.S., Sherali, H.D. and Shetty, C.M. (1993). *Nonlinear Programming Theory and Algorithms*, 2nd edn. New York: Wiley.

Bellman, R. (1957). *Dynamic Programming*. Princeton, N.J: Princeton University Press.

Belton, V. and Vickers, S.P. (1993). 'Demystifying DEA – a visual interactive approach based on multiple criteria analysis', *Journal of the Operational Research Society*, 44, pp. 883–96.

Bodington, C.E. and Baker, T.E. (1990). 'A history of mathematical programming in the petroleum industry', *Interfaces*, 20, pp. 117–27.

Brearley, A.L. Mitra, G. and Williams, H.P. (1975). 'Analysis of mathematical programming problems prior to applying the Simplex algorithm'. *Mathematical Programming*, 8, pp. 54–83.

Butler, T. and Mazzola, J. (1996). 'Improving service productivity – integer programming helps to improve the layout of a parts distribution centre', *OR Insight*, 9:1, pp. 2–7.

Camanho, A.S. and Dyson, R.G. (1990). 'Efficiency, size, benchmarks and targets for bank branches: an application of data envelopment analysis' *Journal of the Operational Research Society*, 50, pp. 903, 915.

Charnes, A. Cooper, W.W. and Rhodes, E. (1978). 'Measuring the efficiency of decision making units'. *European Journal of Operational Research*, 2, pp. 429–44.

Dessent, G. and Hume, B. (1990). 'Value for money and prison perimeters – goal-programming for gaols'. *Journal of the Operational Research Society*, 41, pp. 583–90.

G.W. Evans and R. Fairburn, 'Selection and scheduling of advanced mission for NASA using 0-1 integer linear programming', *Journal of the Operational Research Society*, 40 (1989), pp 971–81

Gould, N.I.M. and Reid, J.K. (1989). 'New crash procedures for large systems of linear constraints'. *Mathematical Programming*, 45, pp. 475-503.

Greeberg, H.J. and Murphy, F.H. (1992). 'A comparison of mathematical programming modeling systems'. *Annals of Operations Research*, 5, pp. 177–238.

Hendry, L.C., Fok, K.K. and Shek, K.W. (1996). 'A cutting stock and scheduling problem in the copper industry'. *Journal of the Operational Research Society*, 47, pp. 38–47.

Hobbs, J. and Neebe, A. (1995). 'Contracting for coal: an integer programming model helps minimise distribution costs at Carolina Power and Lighting Company'. *OR Insight*, 8:1, pp. 28-32.

Koksalan, M. and Sural, H. (1999). 'Efes Beverage Group makes location and distribution desciions for its malt plants'. *Interfaces*, 29, pp. 89–103.

Ozcan, Y.A. and McCue, M.J. (1996). 'Development of a financial performance index for hospitals: DEA approach'. *Journal of the Operational Research Society*, 47, pp. 18–26

Letchford, A. (1996). 'Allocation of school bus contracts using integer programming'. *Journal of the Operational Research Society*, 47, pp. 369–72.

Miliotis, P.A. (1992). 'Data envelopment analysis applied to electricity distribution districts'. *Journal of the Operational Research Society*, 43, pp.549–55.

Nemhauser, G.L. (1994). 'The Age of Optimization: solving large scale real world problems'. *Operations Research*, 42, pp. 5–13.

Romero, C. (1991). *Handbook of Critical Issues in Goal Programming*. Oxford: Pergamon Press.

Stone, P.D. (1996). 'DEA in a major bank'. In Targett, D. *Analytical Decision Making*. London: Pitman Publishing.

Thanassoulis, E., Dyson, R.G. and Foster, M.J. (1987). 'Relative efficiency assessments using data envelopment analysis: an application to data on rates departments'. *Journal of the Operational Research Society*, 38, pp. 397–412.

White, D.J. (1990). 'A bibliography on the applications of mathematical programming multiple-objective methods'. *Journal of the Operational Research Society*, 41, pp. 669–91.

Williams, H.P. (1993). *Model Building in Mathematical Programming*, 3rd edn. Chichester, UK: John Wiley and Sons.

Exercises

Exercises 1–4 can be solved using a graphical approach or a computer-based approach. Exercises 5–8 will need either the Simplex approach or use of a computer solution package.

1. Return to the basic profit maximization problem that we introduced in Chapter 2. Reformulate this as a revenue maximizing problem. Find the optimal solution and complete a full sensitivity analysis.

2. A company purchases crude oil on the open market and refines it into either petrol (P) or diesel (D) fuel for sale in its chain of petrol stations. Under existing market conditions the company makes £20 profit per unit of petrol and £25 per unit of diesel. The company uses three resources in refining: land, labour and capital. Supplies of the three resources are fixed in the short term at 250 units, 2400 units and 1200 units respectively. To refine a unit of petrol requires 2 units of capital, 6 of labour and 0.4 of land. Diesel requires 3, 3 and 0.25 units respectively.

   Formulate this as an LP problem. Find the optimal solution and undertake a sensitivity analysis.

3. The students' union café offers a vegetarian alternative to the hamburger, the BigMik. These burgers come in two sizes, standard (S) and large (L). Both are made from two basic ingredients at the start of each day: a soybean mix and a vegetable/seasoning mix. Any made-up burgers not used are thrown away at the end of the day. A standard veggieburger needs 100 grams of the soybean mix and 50 grams of the vegetable/seasoning mix. A large veggieburger needs 150 grams and 25 grams. The burgers sell at £1 and £1.30 respectively and cost £0.50 and £0.60. The café manager is trying to decide how many of each type of veggieburger to make each day. In addition, she knows that 10 kilos of soybean mix and 4 kilos of vegetable mix are bought each day as are 100 bread buns. Daily demand is for at least 50 standard burgers and at least 10 large.

(a) Formulate and solve this problem as profit maximization. Undertake a sensitivity analysis.
(b) Formulate and solve this problem as cost minimization. Undertake a sensitivity analysis.

4. A company produces breakfast cereals for sale in supermarkets. The cereal is marketed under two brands: the Hifibre and the Nutti. Both cereals are sold in 400g packets and both are made from the same ingredients:

Ingredients	Hifibre	Nutti
Oats and fibre	300 g	250 g
Nuts and fruit	100 g	150 g

The company has a long-term contract to buy weekly supplies of the two ingredients to a maximum of: 1500kg of oats/fibre and 500kg of nuts/fruit. Historically, weekly sales have never exceeded 4000 packets of both products. Sales of Nutti have usually been at least 1000 packets each week. The firm makes a profit of 25p per packet of Hifibre and 35p for Nutti.

Determine the optimal combination of production. What other information can you give the company?

5. A company manufactures five products, A–E, using supplies of raw materials which then go through a three stage production process. The summary data for the five products is:

Table E1 Raw materials for Exercise 5

Product	Raw material required: kg	Time required in stage I (hours)	Time required in stage II (hours)	Time required in stage II (hours)	Selling price per unit (£)
A	6	1	3	0.5	10
B	6.5	0.75	4.5	0.5	10.5
C	6.1	1.25	6	0.5	11
D	6.1	1	6	0.75	12
E	6.4	1	4.5	1	10.5
Maximum supply available	35 000 kg	6 000 hours	30 000 hours	4 000 hours	

Formulate this as an LP problem, solve and interpret the results.

6. A client has come to your financial investment company with £500 000 to invest. The client has asked that you invest the amount in four types of investment:

   G – Government bonds currently producing 8 per cent return per annum

   C – Corporate bonds, 9 per cent return per annum

   S – Shares of companies in the service sector, 10 per cent per annum

   M – Shares of companies in the manufacturing sector, 8 per cent per annum

   The client has asked that:

   • The amount invested in corporate bonds should be at least 10 per cent of the total.
   • The amount invested in government bonds should be at least 40 per cent of the total.
   • No more than half the amount should be invested in manufacturing shares.
   • Total shares should be at least half of the amount invested.
   • The amount invested in service company shares should be more than that in manufacturing company shares.

   How much should be invested in the four alternatives? What further advice would you give your client?

7. A company manufactures four hi-tech products for use in the computer industry. Each product goes through a 4-stage production process:

   Table E2 *Exercise 7: 4-stage production process: time required (mins) per unit produced*

Product	A	B	C	D	Production time available (mins)
Stage 1	1	2	2	1	2500
Stage 2	2	3	1	3	4000
Stage 3	4	2	3	2	4500
Stage 4	0.5	0.5	1	0.5	1200

   At present the company has a contract for weekly production of at least 200 units of A, 150 of B, 300 of C and 200 of D. It receives a price of £25 for each unit of A, £30 for B, £20 for C and £22 for D.

(a) Formulate and solve the problem.

(b) The company's accountant has indicated that the company needs to generate an income of at least £42 000 per week to remain viable. Advise the company.

(c) The company's chief executive has never heard of LP. Explain in non-technical terms how it works for this company.

8. From your own experience describe some situations in organizations where you think LP could be applied.

9. What do you think the main reasons would be for an organization not to use linear programming in its decision-making?

What could be done about these?

Solutions

1. The formulation is as for the profit maximization problem but with an objective function: Max. 39.9B + 44.9D.

The optimal solution is as before with B = 330 and D = 640 but with the OF now £41 903. Sensitivity analysis shows two binding constraints. Cutting has an opportunity cost of £5.54 and could vary from 1950 to 6900. Sewing has an opportunity cost of £2.91 and could vary from 3220 to 7960. The objective function coefficients could vary from £22.45 to £89.8 for B and £19.95 to £79.80 for D.

2. The formulation is:

$$\text{Max. } 20P + 25D$$
$$\text{s.t.}$$
$$0.4P + 0.25D \leq 250$$
$$6P + 3D \leq 2400$$
$$2P + 3D \leq 1200$$

The solution is found as:

Profit £11 000
P = 300
D = 200

Labour and capital constraints are binding, 80 units of land are unused.

Sensitivity analysis on the objective function indicates that the profit coefficient for P can vary from 16.667 to 50 without affecting the current solution and that of D from 10 to 30. Sensitivity analysis on the binding constraints gives an opportunity cost of 0.837 for labour and 7.5 for capital. Other things being equal, it would be more profitable to acquire extra supplies of capital. The range of variation for labour is between 1200 to 3600 and for capital between 800 to 2400. This implies an additional 1200 units of capital would be worthwhile obtaining.

3 (a) The formulation is:

$$\text{Max. } 0.5S + 0.7L$$
$$\text{s.t.}$$
$$0.1S + 0.15L \leq 10$$
$$0.05S + 0.025L \leq 4$$
$$1S + 1L \leq 100$$
$$1S \geq 50$$
$$1L \geq 10$$

with a solution

$$\text{Profit} = £49$$
$$S = 70$$
$$L = 10$$

Sensitivity analysis indicates that constraints 1 and 2, relating to the supplies of the two ingredients, are binding. Twenty of the 100 bread buns bought each day are not required. The objective function coefficients have a range of 0.467 to 1.4 for S and 0.25 to 0.75 for L. The ranges indicate the change in the respective profit contributions before the optimal solution changes. Constraint 1 has an opportunity cost of 4.5 and a range from 9 to 12, whilst constraint 2 has an opportunity cost of 1 and a range of 3.3 to 4.5. Other things being equal, additional supplies of the soybean mix should be obtained.

3 (b) The formulation is:

Min. 0.5S + 0.6L
s.t.
0.1S + 0.15L ≤ 10
0.05S + 0.025L ≤ 4
1S + 1L ≤ 100
1S ≥ 50
1L ≥ 10

with a solution

Profit = £31
S = 50
L = 10

and constraints 1 and 2 binding. Sensitivity analysis on the objective function indicates that both decision variables can vary their coefficients from 0 to infinity. Constraint 4 (relating to the minimum quantity of S) has an opportunity cost of 0.50 and a range of 0 to 75. Constraint 5 (relating to the minimum quantity of L) has an opportunity cost of 0.60 and a range of 0 to 33.

4. The formulation is:

Max 25H + 35N
s.t.
300H + 250N ≤ 150 000
100H + 150N ≤ 50 000
1H + 1N ≤ 4000
1N ≥ 1000

H,N ≥ 0

Note that the formulation could also express the objective function in £'s rather than pence and the first two constraints in kg rather than g.

The solution gives H=2000, N=2000 and profit at £1200 per week. Constraints 2 and 3 are binding. There are 400 kg of oats/fibre not required each week. Sensitivity analysis on the OF indicates that the coefficient for H can vary from 23.3p to 35p without altering the current optimal solution. The permitted range for N is 25p to 37.5p.

Opportunity costs for constraints 2 and 3 are 0.2p and 5p respectively. The first indicates that additional supplies of nuts/fruit would be profitable. the second indicates that it would be even more profitable to change the maximum production constraint from its current limit of 4000 packets. Constraint 2 has a range of 459kg to 6000kg and Constraint 3 a range of 3333.3kg to 4500kg.

5. The formulation is:

$$\text{Max } 10A + 10.5B + 11C + 12D + 10.5E$$
$$\text{s.t.}$$
$$6A + 6.5B + 6.1C + 6.1D + 6.4E \leq 35\,000$$
$$1A + 0.75B + 1.25C + 1D + 1E \leq 6000$$
$$3A + 4.5B + 6C + 6D + 4.5E \leq 30\,000$$
$$0.5A + 0.5B + 0.5C + 0.75D + 1E \leq 4000$$

The solution is to produce 1525.4 units of A and 4237.3 units of D at a profit of £66101.69. Constraints one and three are binding indicating excess supply of stages I and III hours. Sensitivity analysis on the binding constraints gives an opportunity cost of 1.356 for constraint 1 and 0.621 for constraint 3. The maximum increase in constraint 1 is to 36 400 kg. Sensitivity analysis on the objective function indicates that A's coefficient could vary from £8.42 to £11.8 and that of D from £11 to £20. The analysis also reveals that the selling price of the non-basic products would need to be £11.6 for B, £12 for C and £11.47 for E before it became worthwhile including them in the optimal solution.

6. The formulation is:

$$\text{Max. } 0.08G + 0.09C + 0.10S + 0.08M$$
$$\text{s.t.}$$
$$1G + 1C + 1S + 1M \leq 500\,000$$
$$1M \leq 125\,000$$
$$1C \geq 50\,000$$
$$1G \geq 200\,000$$
$$1S + 1M \geq 250\,000$$
$$1S - 1M > 0$$

the solution indicates investments of:

G	£200 000
C	£50 000
S	£250 000

and that this will generate a return of £45 500 per annum.

The sensitivity analysis reveals that the client's constraints are having a detrimental effect on the return generated. In particular, constraint 4 relating to the requirement that G be at least 40 per cent of the total investment reduces the overall return by 2 per cent (0.02). That is, by requiring an investment of at least £200 000 in G which has a return of 8 per cent we are preventing further investment in S with a return of 10 per cent.

7 (a) The formulation is:

$$\text{Max. } 25A + 30B + 20C + 22D$$
s.t.
$$1A + 2B + 2C + 1D \le 2500$$
$$2A + 3B + 1C + 3D \le 4000$$
$$4a + 2B + 3C + 2D < 4500$$
$$0.5A + 0.5B + 1C + 0.5D \le 1200$$
$$1A \ge 200$$
$$1B \ge 150$$
$$1C > 300$$
$$1D \ge 200$$

The solution generates an income of £41 725 per week and requires:
$$A = 425$$
$$B = 525$$
$$C = 300$$
$$D = 425$$

Constraints 1–3 are binding.

7 (b) Given that the optimal solution generates an income of only £41 725 whilst £42 000 is required, then some change is required to the business. From the sensitivity analysis a number of possibilities arise. One is to acquire additional time for Stage 1 of the process. This has an opportunity cost of £8 and an additional 225 minutes could be obtained

without affecting the current solution, thus generating additional revenue of £1800 per week.

Alternatively, there is a high opportunity cost of £7.375 for constraint 7, which requires production of C to be at least 300 units. The implication is that requiring production of C is restraining income and, according to our solution, C could be reduced by 138.5 units without affecting the current solution. The company may be able to renegotiate this contract with its customers. Alternatively, it could consider contracting this part of its work out to another company if the cost of this were less than £27.375 (the existing revenue from C plus the opportunity cost).

Critical Path Analysis

Jonathan H. Klein

7 | Introduction

7.1 Projects

A great deal of human activity, and in particular organizational activity, can be characterized as taking the form of *projects*. A project is an assembly of people and resources intended to achieve, by means of various activities, the attainment of a specific objective over a period of time. All but the simplest of projects involve appreciable numbers of activities, people, and resources. Therefore, projects require the organization and management of these activities, people and resources.

The idea of a project is fairly ubiquitous in human life. At the domestic level, countless activities can be characterized as projects. Two obvious examples include preparing a meal or cleaning a house. It is quite easy to see how these activities can be regarded as projects. For example, preparing a meal requires a fairly specific notion of the desired end result, a variety of ingredients, and a number of activities that must be carried out by one or more people in order to transform the ingredients into the meal, usually within a specified time period. But other activities can also, less obviously, be regarded as projects, such as planning and taking a holiday, or educating one's children.

University students on teaching programmes, both at the undergraduate and postgraduate level, generally undertake projects as part of their studies. These consist of various different activities, have deadlines, and require resources, such as students' time and effort. A research student undertaking PhD studies is essentially embarking upon a project, and the process of studying for a qualification at university can, similarly, be regarded as a project.

Business organizations frequently undertake projects. For example, motor car manufacturers undertake projects to design, build and manufacture new models of car. Building contractors of all sizes undertake construction projects of varying complexity. Many types of organization undertake research and development

(R&D) projects. Activities as diverse as organizational restructuring, opening up new markets, and planning strategic direction can all be usefully characterized as projects.

Projects are, of course, not confined to the private sector. Public sector organizations undertake projects. Government departments, and even government itself, undertake projects.

Increasingly, organizations are viewing a larger proportion of even the routine activities they undertake as projects. Gilbreath (1988) argues that this *'projectization'* of work is particularly suited to the modern business climate, characterized as it is by 'the phenomena of rapid social, economic, technological, and political change'. He argues that 'in times of change the project orientation dominates all operational frameworks', and that 'perceptive managers know ... that in times of change, for today and tomorrow, they will more often than not be managing projects' (p. 3). A recent extensive study of European organizations (Whittington *et al.* 1999) found that in the period from 1992 to 1996 'project-based structures became more pervasive, with 51 per cent of firms placing a greater emphasis on them in 1996 compared to 1992; 42 per cent of firms placed much or greater emphasis on project structures in 1996, against only 13 per cent in 1992'. Morris (1994) comments: 'major industrial companies now use project management as their principal management style. "Management by projects" has become a powerful way to integrate organizational functions and motivate groups to achieve higher levels of performance and productivity' (p. 1).

Some projects are enormous, and consequently very visible. Recent examples in the UK include the construction of the Channel Tunnel and the privatization of the railways. Beyond the UK, prominent projects include the US space programme and the reunification of Germany.

It should be clear that many projects are very complex indeed. If they are to run properly (that is, if they are to achieve what they are intended to achieve) they need to be managed formally. Informal management, which might be good enough for small-scale domestic projects, where things are relatively simple, and the stakes are relatively low, will not be good enough.

This text describes a class of techniques developed during the twentieth century which have been designed to aid the management of complex projects. The aim of the techniques is to provide a way of describing projects which enables project managers to gain an appreciation of the component activities and required resources for their projects. This enables them to do a number of things. It enables them to plan the way in which the activities will be co-ordinated and the resources brought to bear. It enables them to estimate how long the project will take, and what resources it is likely to require. It enables them to investigate alternative plans, for example trading off the duration of the project (which, generally, managers would want to minimize) against resource consumption (which they would also generally wish to minimize). It enables them to have a standard against which to monitor actual project progress and make changes, in an informed way, as the project proceeds. Finally, at the end of the project, it enables them to document the project and its progress in a way which, hopefully, will inform the planning of future projects.

The techniques are based on graphical representations of the component activities. Activities are represented as lines on a diagram. The lines are linked together according to particular conventions, in order to represent the way in which the activities are related to each other over time. Thus, the graphical representations are *networks* of lines representing activities. Such graphical representations provide easy-to-read pictures of projects. When combined with mathematical representation of quantitative features of the activities, such as their duration or resource usage, the representations constitute a powerful method of planning projects.

The method can be used to plan projects which consist of many thousands of component activities. For projects with this kind of magnitude (or even with just a hundred or so activities), manual use of the technique becomes impractical and computer assistance is almost a necessity. However, for small projects, consisting of a few activities, manual use is perfectly feasible, and may even be preferable to automated use. This book explains the mathematical techniques. They are very straightforward in themselves (amounting to little more than the disciplined use of simple arithmetic) though, as the number of activities increases, it becomes increasingly impractical to do the arithmetic manually. Still, it is worth knowing, both for dealing with simple cases, because an appreciation of what computer software does can be valuable, and to prevent misinterpretation and misuse of computer results.

The techniques described in this book were developed for use in large scale projects, where management and co-ordination of activities is an important issue, and often constitutes a serious problem. However, it is my contention (and that of many others) that the techniques also have value in relatively simple contexts, such as the domestic or personal, where hitherto purely informal methods might have been used. Boothroyd (1978) cites the example of a shopping trip undertaken by himself and his wife in which a ten-minute 'back-of-an-envelope' piece of network analysis enabled them to complete, with time to spare, what initially seemed like an infeasible quantity of tasks. The story may or may not be apocryphal, but it is very credible. I work at an institution where we try to practice what we preach: at the School of Management of the University of Southampton, as in many other higher education institutions, both staff and students are encouraged to prepare network-related *Gantt charts* (graphical representations of schedules, sometimes known as *schedule graphs*) and similar aids when proposing, planning and monitoring projects. Generally, the time taken to do so is well spent.

7.2 Characteristics of projects

Extrapolating from the discussion above, it is possible to assemble a list of features which projects generically possess. In some projects some of these features may be fairly minimal. It can be argued that, for large and costly projects, all these features *should* be well-defined, though I am reluctant to be too prescriptive.

The generic features of a project are:

- A project has objectives which are supposed to be achieved. In the simplest cases, these are defined at the outset of the project. But in many projects, the objectives may be refined or changed as the projects proceed. Achievement of the objectives is generally equated to the success of the project.
- There are generally a number of criteria which inform the definition of project objectives. Many authorities cite the 'trinity' of cost (to be minimized), duration (to be minimized) and quality (to be maximized), and argue that good project management requires successful trading-off between these criteria (see, for example, Maylor 1999). Turner (1993) presents a more sophisticated picture, in which a fourth criterion, the scope of the project, is added, and in which trade-offs are therefore potentially more complex.

- A project consists of a number of distinct component activities. This number may range from the very small to many thousands.
- The sequence of activities in a project is by no means arbitrary. For example, generally you cannot build the walls of a building before you have laid the foundations.
- However, there is usually a degree of flexibility in the way in which project activities are sequenced, which gives rise to alternative options for the plan of a project.
- Project activities require resources in order to be carried out. In particular, an activity requires the time and effort of the person (or persons) who is (or are) to carry it out. Other resources might include money, materials or personnel with specialist skills.
- Project activities have durations associated with them. The duration of an activity is the period of time between the start of the activity and its completion. In general, this is not the same as the time required of a person to carry it out. For example, I may be able to devote five hours a week to writing a text which I estimate will require a total of fifty hours writing time. Then, the duration of the activity will be ten weeks (assuming I take no breaks in my schedule). The distinction between duration and required time is an important one. It is a fairly obvious distinction, but there is potential for confusion.
- The resource requirements of project activities constrain the way in which the activities are arranged. For example, if you are the sole person carrying out the activities, there is a limit to the number of activities you can carry out at the same time (according to my wife, my limit is one!).
- There may be flexibility in the amount of resource a project activity requires. For example, the duration of some activities can be reduced by spending more money on them (hiring additional labour for a building activity, for example). This leads to the possibility of trading off different features of a project (project duration versus project cost, for example), and possible alternative plans.
- Ultimately, the definition of a project is subjective. Whether you choose to view a set of activities as a project is up to you. If you do, some advantages will accrue, such as the opportunity to apply project management techniques such as those described in this book. For large-scale enterprises where one is charged with using resources responsibly the advantages are substantial and hard to reject. However, for smaller enterprises (domestic and

personal, for example) the advantages are correspondingly less, and some might argue (though I am not sure that I would) that there are disadvantages against which they should be weighed. Two such disadvantages that are sometimes cited are: a stifling of creativity in the way one goes about things; and, diversion of time and effort from doing whatever one is supposed to be doing into managing its doing.

7.3 An introductory example: planning and monitoring a research project

I shall continue this introductory chapter with a brief example of the use of the kind of techniques described in this book. Because the example is simple, and because of the particular situation, the analysis is conducted informally, rather than with the aid of mathematical methods. However, the principles are the same. It is a realistic example, from my own personal experience.

From time to time I am approached, as a management scientist in the employ of a university, to undertake projects for outside organizations such as businesses or governmental departments. There are a variety of good reasons why such organizations might approach the academic community. Typically such projects are part consultancy (they involve carrying out specific studies for the client organizations, to fulfil specific purposes) and part research (they involve developing new ideas, or using current ideas in new ways). As such, they fall within the realm of appropriate activities for a university to undertake, and they also help fund the university. (An increasing proportion of a UK university's income comes from such activities rather than teaching.)

Typically, when an organization approaches me, I set up a meeting between myself (I am assuming that I shall be working alone on the project, which is by no means always the case) and representatives of the client organization. At this meeting, my prospective clients would describe their problem as thoroughly as possible. It would then be up to me to develop a proposal describing the work I would undertake, how long it would take, and what it would cost. This proposal would take the form of a short document. Somewhere in the document there would be a *Gantt chart*. Many, if not most, clients would expect to find such a graph in the proposal.

To compile the Gantt chart, I would consider the component activities of the project. For a typical project involving studying a particular function undertaken by the organization and making recommendations as to how it might be changed (hopefully for the better), the component activities might be:

- *Literature search:* study the literature on the function, and, if appropriate, consult experts in the field.
- *Field study:* observe current organizational practice, and talk to representatives of the organization.
- *Preliminary report:* write a report which describes the results of the literature search and the field study, and outlines a way to proceed, and submit this report to the client organization.
- *Client discussion:* discuss the contents of the preliminary report with client representatives, and agree a way to proceed (either the one recommended in the report, or a renegotiated one).
- *Final report:* proceed as agreed, developing a set of recommendations, and submit to client as a final written report.
- *Presentation:* present the report to the client and revise in the light of client comments.

How long might each activity take? The way I normally estimate activity durations in this type of project is to assume that I have a fixed amount of time available per week, after other academic duties have been carried out. Suppose this to be one working day. Then I would estimate the amount of my time required for each activity, in working days. I might estimate the literature search, for example, as requiring eight working days. So I'd expect the duration of the literature search to be eight weeks, assuming I was devoting my day per week entirely to it. Similar estimates can be made for the other activities. In Table 7.1 I have listed the activities, assigned each a code letter, and tabulated their labour requirements in person-days.

Table 7.1 Component activities for the consultancy project.

Activity code	Description of activity	Person-days required
A	Literature search	8
B	Field study	4
C	Preliminary report	4
D	Client discussion	2
E	Final report	12
F	Presentation	2

At first sight, it might appear that all the activities should be carried out in series, one after the other. In fact, this is not the case. Some activities can be carried out in parallel. For example, for a variety of reasons I would probably wish to start the field study while carrying out the literature review. Clearly, at any given moment in time I would not be doing both, but in a particular week I might be engaged on both activities. However, if I were to give up some of my weekly allocated time for the literature review to the field study, clearly the duration of the literature review will be longer than it would be otherwise (and, of course, the duration of the field study would be longer than if I were solely doing it). I am assuming that each activity will require the same amount of my time, no matter whether or not I carry it out in parallel with other activities. This is a fairly safe and accurate assumption in this case.

In order to represent the way in which I might organize the project activities, I would construct a Gantt chart. Figure 7.1 shows such a chart.

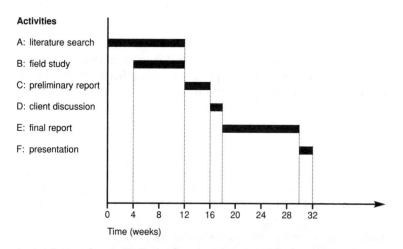

Figure 7.1 Gantt chart (or schedule graph) for the consultancy project

In the Gantt chart, the horizontal axis represents time. In Figure 7.1, time is demarcated in weeks, and simply referred to in terms of the number of weeks elapsed since the start of the project at time 0.

On the vertical axis of the graph are the six component activities of the project. For each activity, I have drawn a line representing the span of time over which the activity is scheduled to run. For example, Activity A, the literature review, spans the first twelve weeks of the project. This activity is now taking longer than eight weeks, because Activity B is running in parallel with it. For similar reasons, Activity B requires eight weeks instead of four. This means that I shall have to divide my one person-day per week between Activities A and B for eight weeks. Effectively, I have argued that Activity A, requiring eight person-days, will receive one person-day per week for the first four weeks, and half a person-day per week for the next eight weeks. Similarly, Activity B, requiring four person-days, will receive half a person-day per week for eight weeks.

As far as the rest of the activities are concerned, they run in series. I have argued that I cannot start writing my preliminary report (Activity C) until both the literature review and the field study (Activities A and B) are completed, and, by similar arguments, that the subsequent activities must proceed serially. In total, the duration of the entire project is 32 weeks.

I could, of course, have chosen to carry out Activities A and B one after the other, too, rather than partially in parallel. In theory this should not alter the duration of the project. I should merely be redistributing the way I allocate my one day per week. However, I have chosen to run the two activities in parallel to give me a bit more flexibility. I doubt that I shall spend exactly half a day on each in all the eight weeks they are scheduled to run in parallel, but bearing in mind that the field study will require liaising with my client, and that some of the literature I shall want to look at may take some time to obtain, it would help to have some degree of manoeuvre in exactly how to conduct these activities.

Activities A, C and E will be conducted by myself alone. The other Activities, B, D and F require input from my client. Thus it is worth pointing out to my client when these inputs will be required, and that failure to receive these inputs will have a knock-on effect that will delay the entire project. I am particularly concerned about the field study. If I am unable to negotiate the necessary access to my client in the available time, this will delay the project. One way of alleviating this effect would be to commence the field study immediately, so that it is scheduled to run, in parallel with the literature review, over the first eight weeks of the project. This means that it would be scheduled to end four weeks before the end of the literature review. Since both the literature review and the field study must be complete before I can begin writing the preliminary report, this means that I would have four weeks 'in reserve' by which the field study could be delayed before it impacted on the total duration of the project.

I might also wish to amend the schedule to take into account the fact that I do not expect to be able to devote one day per week every week. This involves switching from a time-scale measured in project time to a time-scale measured in calendar time. For example, my client and I are currently negotiating for a start date at the beginning of October 2000. I intend to take a two week break at the end of December (corresponding to project weeks 13 and 14). So the project would not progress in these two weeks, and the total calendar duration would be thirty-four weeks. If the project starts at the beginning of October, it should be concluded by the end of May. However, my teaching schedule gets far lighter towards June, and thus I would be able to devote more time per week to the project in June and July. Thus, I could point out to my clients that a delay of a month or so in starting the project would not necessarily lead to the same delay in its completion. We could use the Gantt chart to explore such possibilities.

Then there is the question of costing the project. I would use a standard person-day rate, and multiply this by the number of person-days I estimate the project to require: 32, in this case.

My client and I could also negotiate project 'milestones', whereby we can check how the project is progressing. For example, by the end of the sixteenth week, the preliminary report should be complete. This might be an appropriate milestone which my client could use to gauge that progress is satisfactory, and, possibly, release a payment based on work to date (that is, Activities A, B and C). However, it is likely that I would consult the activity schedule more frequently during the progress of the project (maybe every week or so) and decide whether activities have progressed broadly according to schedule. If they have, or if they appear to be ahead, fine. If they are behind schedule, I need to take some action: devote more time to the project, or, if the problem lies with non-cooperation of the client, advise the client of the problem, or, if all else fails, prepare to report to the client that I am behind schedule and, possibly, renegotiate the schedule.

In summary, the Gantt chart has provided, in concise, easily understandable form, an aid which has enabled me, either alone, or in negotiation with my client, to determine:

- The component activities of the project and the amount of resource (principally my time, but also input from my client) to be expended on each.
- A schedule for the activities, indicating when they should start and finish, and when they should run in parallel, observing that some activities cannot begin until others have been completed.
- Those activities which, if they are delayed, would delay the entire project.
- An activity (the field study) which, by being scheduled earlier, ceases to threaten the duration of the project.
- How other considerations, such as holidays or my teaching schedule, might affect the duration of the project, and the implications of different start dates.
- Milestones which I can offer to the client as a means of monitoring my progress.
- A schedule which I can use to monitor my own progress, with a view to correcting poor progress if need be.
- A basis for costing the project.

The graph acts as a device for enabling me to both reflect effectively upon the project and communicate effectively with my client concerning the project. I have discussed the undoubted value of diagrammatic representations in general elsewhere (Klein 1994).

For this project, with only six activities, it is hardly necessary to resort to formal mathematical analysis. Simple commonsense more or less gets me there. For larger projects (that is, ones with more activities) common sense analysis will not suffice. More formal aids are required. The remainder of this book discusses such aids. However, it should be appreciated that what these aids provide is nothing more – or less – than a systematic means of going about the types of analysis that have been described in an informal setting above. In complex situations, common sense alone is not enough. We also need a systematic approach to applying it, and, quite possibly, automated aids for carrying out the work in a reasonable span of time.

7.4 Structure of the text

This chapter has introduced the topic of critical path analysis techniques, and, hopefully, demonstrated their value by means of a simple but realistic example. The remainder of this book discusses critical path analysis techniques in more detail.

Chapter 8 describes the mathematical theory of critical path methods. This is introduced by means of a straightforward example and standard graphical representations of the methods. This chapter should provide an understanding of the mathematics of critical path analysis, and enable the reader to undertake manual analysis of small projects consisting of a few activities.

For larger projects, the use of computer software is practically essential. Chapter 9 discusses the characteristics of critical path software, and reviews the software that is commercially available.

Chapter 10 discusses the use of critical path methods in practice. In particular, the chapter addresses how the use of the methods fits in with project management more generally.

Chapter 11 briefly discusses the literature relating to critical path analysis techniques.

Finally, Chapter 12 concludes the text by discussing the future of critical path analysis techniques.

8 Critical Path Network Analysis Techniques

8.1 Introduction

Critical path network analysis techniques are a set of fairly straightforward mathematically-based tools designed to facilitate project planning and monitoring. The approach models a project as a schedule of interconnected component activities. This schedule can be represented as a graphical network.

At its most basic, critical path modelling enables a time schedule for the component activities of a project to be developed and monitored. However, the models are generally enhanced to include consideration of the consumption of other resources than time, such as money.

In this chapter, we shall present the mathematical theory of critical path methods. These theoretical principles are straightforward and mathematically elementary. Use of the methods amounts to little more than the systematic use of basic arithmetic operations. Graphical representation of the methods, which we shall make use of, enhances this straightforwardness.

While the methods are extremely straightforward, applying them effectively to large projects which contain many component activities requires the use of a computer and appropriate software. Such software is today routinely available for use on personal computers (PCs), and we shall return to consider it in Chapter 9. It should, however, be noted that the existence of this software does not obviate the need for the user to have some real understanding of the underlying theory. Reviewing a selection of PC software packages available commercially, Maroto and Tormos (1994) have commented: 'it is essential to have previous knowledge of scheduling techniques and project control for an appropriate use of … management packages. The documentation the packages provide, even those of the highest quality, does not make up for this fact' (p. 220). More generally, knowledge and understanding of the underlying theory enables users of computer implementations to

119

understand the strengths and the limitations of the approach they are using, and to work with more confidence. An ability to use critical path techniques manually also enables one to sketch out plans for projects with few component activities. Such projects may be genuinely small ones. But it is often useful, for a variety of reasons, to consider large projects as being composed of relatively few 'macro' activities, each of which is an aggregate of many smaller 'micro' component activities.

Much of the formal theory underlying critical path methods was developed during the 1950s, although informal graphical techniques had already been in use as project management aids for several decades. Because similar techniques were developed more or less independently, there is a variety of notation and terminology, the precise meaning of which may vary from user to user. Two terms, in particular, are in very common usage: the *critical path method* (CPM), and the *project evaluation and review technique* (PERT). These terms are sometimes used to refer to the general body of network-based scheduling techniques, and sometimes to specific variations. In this book, we follow a fairly common convention, and use the term CPM to refer to the general body of techniques, while we use the term PERT to refer to a specific variation concerned with modelling the uncertainty of component activity durations.

In the next section of this chapter (Section 8.2) the basic critical path network technique, for modelling networks of activities in which all activity durations are assumed to be known with certainty, is introduced. The section shows how the timings of individual activities, and the duration of the entire project, may be determined. Section 8.3 introduces the Gantt chart representation. Section 8.4 demonstrates how uncertainty of activity durations may be incorporated within a network model. In Section 8.5, the trading-off of activity durations and costs is briefly considered. Section 8.6 considers how schedules may be designed which take into account the usage of resources other than time.

8.2 The critical path method (CPM)

The fundamental critical path analysis technique is the *critical path method* (CPM). This approach models a project as a graphical network of inter-related component activities. It is assumed that the duration of each activity is known with certainty. The method enables its user to establish:

- The minimum time in which the project can be completed.
- Which activities may be executed at the same time.
- Which activities are *critical*, meaning that a delay in any one of them is bound to cause a delay to the entire project.
- Which activities are not critical, meaning that some time-slack is available for their completion.

8.2.1 Work breakdown structure (WBS)

Critical path analysis requires that the component activities of the project under consideration must be identified, together with their durations. The component activities of a project may be identified using a *work breakdown structure* (WBS). A WBS is a decomposition of a project into a hierarchy of component activities. The top level consists of just one overall activity: the entire project. At the next level down, this is decomposed into a number of component activities, which are, in turn, further decomposed at the next level down. This process of successive decomposition through successively lower levels continues until there is no longer anything to be gained from further decomposition.

To illustrate this idea, we introduce an example. The *EBSP Detector Project* (I once constructed an EBSP detector) is a fairly simple project, with relatively few component activities. However, it is the kind of project which might benefit from the manual use of critical path analysis techniques.

The EBSP Detector Project

Purpose: the design and construction of an electron back-scattering pattern (EBSP) detector for a scanning electron microscope.

Description: A physics laboratory requires a purpose-built electron back-scattering pattern (EBSP) detector for attachment to a scanning electron microscope. The detector needs first to be designed, and then constructed. To design the detector requires an accurate specification of its intended function, a thorough survey of the microscope to determine the physical constraints relating to attachment, identification of possible suppliers of various required parts, gathering of information from suppliers as to what is available, and preparation of a drawing-board design. Construction of the system involves obtaining appropriate parts from suppliers, fabrication of the detector screen, fabrication of the screen mounting, fabrication of the microscope interface, construction of the screen-mounting sub-assembly, construction of the subassembly-interface assembly, and, finally, fitting the assembly to the microscope.

Personnel: the EBSP detector will be designed and constructed by a laboratory technician.

Figure 8.1 shows a WBS for the EBSP Detector Project as developed by the technician responsible for it. The WBS has been developed as a three-level hierarchy. The top level consists of a single activity: the entire project. At the second level, the project has been decomposed into two activities: design and construction. These might be regarded as phases of the project. At the third level, these phases have each been further decomposed into various component operational activities. Note that:

- Each activity is completely equivalent to its component activities at the next level down (that is, in moving to a more detailed description, no parts of the activity have been omitted).
- At any level in the hierarchy, there is no overlap of activities (that is, a piece of work is only specified once at any level).

These two properties should be a feature of any good WBS.

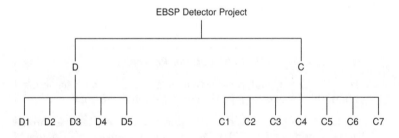

Figure 8.1 A work breakdown structure for the EBSP Detector Project

The activities at the lowest, most detailed, level of the WBS may be used as the component activities of a network model of the project. Table 8.1 lists these activities. Each activity has been given an identification code. The five design phase activities are coded D1 through to D5, and the seven construction phase activities are coded C1 through to C7. Also included in Table 8.1 are the durations, in days, of the activities, as estimated by the technician responsible for the project.

Table 8.1 Activities for the EBSP Detector Project, and their estimated durations

Activity code	Description of activity	Duration (days)
D1	Specification of function	1
D2	Survey of microscope	1
D3	Identification of suppliers	1
D4	Information from suppliers	5
D5	Drawing of design	6
C1	Obtaining parts	5
C2	Fabrication of detector screen	10
C3	Fabrication of mounting	4
C4	Fabrication of interface	8
C5	Construction of subassembly	1
C6	Construction of assembly	1
C7	Fitting	1

Of course, what we have not considered in this description is how the technician chose the structure of Figure 8.1 (as opposed to other possible structures she might have developed), or how she estimated the duration of the low-level activities in it. This is because this chapter is focusing on critical path theory. We shall return to a consideration of these kinds of question in Chapter 10.

The work breakdown structure has other functions in addition to its use in providing initial information for the use of critical path analysis. For example, it can be used to assist in allocating personnel to activities. The wider use of the WBS is discussed in general texts on project management (see, for example, Meredith and Mantel 1995).

8.2.2 Precedence relationships

The activities in Table 8.1 could probably be executed one after the other. However, it is likely that there exists scope for carrying out some of the activities at the same time. In this case, this should not affect the duration of any of the activities. For example, activity C2 (fabrication of detector screen) is scheduled to take ten days. However, this does not imply that it involves ten full days of work. Actually, the amount of work (as with all the activities) is comparatively small, but it involves coating a glass disc with a phosphorescent material, and during parts of this process the disc must be allowed to stand undisturbed for considerable time periods. Thus, the technician will have plenty of time for other things during activity C2, and some of these other things could be other activities to do with the project. A similar argument applies to the other activities in this project. For this project, the time the technician actually spends on the project activities is not a scarce resource. The time the technician spends on an activity is generally very much less than its anticipated duration.

If it is possible to run some activities wholly or partially in parallel, this would clearly allow the duration of the entire project to be shorter than if the activities were run in a strict series. Generally, reducing project duration is regarded as a good and desirable thing (other things being equal). In this case it would enable the EBSP detector to be up and running earlier.

To create a schedule that incorporates the possibility of running activities in parallel, it is necessary to know the *precedence relationships* between the activities: which activities have to be complete before other activities can be started. Table 8.2 presents a set of precedence relationships for the EBSP Detector Project, as identified by the technician. For each activity, the technician has identified the other activities that must be completed before the activity can be started. For example, Table 8.2 indicates that activity D4 (drawing of design) cannot start until activities D2 (survey of microscope) and D4 (information from suppliers) have been completed.

Note that in Table 8.2, logically redundant precedence relationships have been omitted. For example, C1 (obtaining parts) should be preceded by all of the design activities D1, D2, D3, D4 and D5, but by specifying that C1 must be preceded by D5, the other precedences are implied (since the table states that D5 must be preceded by D2 and D4, D4 by D3, and D2 by D1).

8.2.3 Activity-on-node (AON) diagram

Using the information in Table 8.2, it is now straightforward to construct an *activity-on-node* (AON) network diagram for the

Table 8.2 Activity durations and precedence relationships for the EBSP Detector Project

Activity	Duration (days)	Must be preceded by
D1	1	–
D2	1	D1
D3	1	D1
D4	5	D3
D5	6	D2, D4
C1	5	D5
C2	10	D5
C3	4	C1
C4	8	D5
C5	1	C2, C3
C6	1	C4, C5
C7	1	C6

project. In an AON diagram, activities are represented by nodes, and the precedence relationships represented by arrows linking the appropriate node pairs. Conventionally, arrows run (not necessarily horizontally) from left to right across the page (or screen), so that the progress of the project over time roughly corresponds to scanning the diagram from left to right.

Figure 8.2 shows an AON diagram for the EBSP Detector Project, based solely on the information in Table 8.2. Generally, AON diagrams are easy to draw from tables of precedence relationships. Such diagrams nicely illustrate the precedence relationships that exist between activities in a project, and may be valuable for that reason. However, they have little other value except as a stepping stone to a more useful kind of graphical representation.

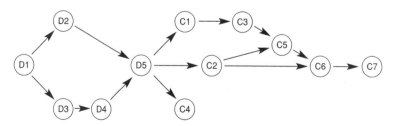

Figure 8.2 An activity-on-node (AON) diagram for the EBSP Detector Project

8.2.4 Activity-on-arrow (AOA) diagram

AON diagrams are relatively easy to draw and to interpret, but the amount of information they can be used to generate is limited. *Activity-on-arrow* (AOA) network diagrams are generally more useful for generating further information. In AOA diagrams, activities are represented by arrows, and the nodes linking the arrows correspond to beginnings and ends of activities.

AOA diagrams are rather more difficult to draw and interpret than AON diagrams. However, they have some important advantages. In an AOA diagram, nodes correspond to the beginnings and ends of activities, and such events are typically used as milestones by which the progress of a project may be measured. Thus, AOA diagrams lend themselves naturally to the process of monitoring and controlling project process in a way that AON diagrams do not. A related point is that AOA diagrams are structurally very closely related to Gantt charts (to be introduced in Section 8.3), which are in wide general usage in project management (and have been for several decades) and are easily interpreted. The logic of AOA construction can be used to inform the preparation of a Gantt chart.

It is possible to draw an AOA diagram directly from a table of precedence information, such as Table 8.2. However, experience suggests that it is easier to draw an AOA diagram working from an AON diagram such as Figure 8.2, rather than working directly from tabulated data. Generally, it is well worth spending a few minutes drawing an AON diagram as a precursor to drawing an AOA diagram.

An AOA diagram should start with a single node representing the start of the project. This node should be placed at the far left of the page (or screen). The arrows representing the initial project activities (those without any predecessors specified) should all start on this node. These arrows should run from left to right. Each arrow should end on a node which then represents the end of the activity corresponding to the arrow. A single node may be the end node for more than one activity: more than one arrow may end on a particular node.

An end node for one or more activities is generally the start node for one or more other activities, as dictated by the logic of the specified precedence relationships. The exception to this is a single end-of-project node, which forms the end node for all final activities of the project (activities which are not specified as predecessors for any other activities).

All nodes in an AOA diagram should be identified by numbers. The start-of-project node should be identified as Node 1. All other nodes should be numbered in such a way that all arrows lead from lower-numbered to higher-numbered nodes (this sometimes allows a choice of number allocation to nodes).

Figure 8.3 shows an AOA diagram for the EBSP Detector Project. In drawing this diagram, the technician worked directly from the AON diagram of Figure 8.2. She started with a start-of-project node at the far left. She drew an arrow representing the initial project activity, D1, which Figure 8.2 indicates to have no precedence requirements. She drew a node at the end of the arrow to represent the end of the activity. Then, noting from Figure 8.2 that D2 and D3 immediately follow D1, she drew two arrows starting on the end node for D1, to represent D2 and D3. She proceeded in this manner through the entire set of activities in Figure 8.2, finishing on an end node. Passing from left to right through the diagram, she numbered the nodes from 1 upwards, so that no arrow finished on a lower number than it started. Finally, she wrote in the duration of each activity (from Table 8.2) next to its corresponding arrow.

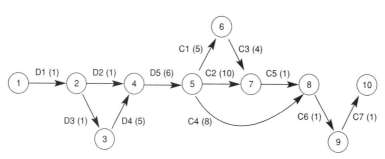

Figure 8.3 An activity-on-arrow (AOA) diagram for the EBSP Detector Project, with activity durations indicated in brackets

8.2.5 Activity timings

An AOA diagram such as that of Figure 8.3 can be used to generate much information about the timing of individual activities in the project. First, we can determine the *earliest start* (ES) time and *earliest finish* (EF) time for each activity, assuming that all preceding activities have been started at their earliest possible times and that they have been completed on time. We do this by making a forward pass (working through the nodes in *ascending* numerical order) through the AOA network, carrying out the following operations:

1. Starting at node 0, assign all activities that start on this node an ES time of 0.
2. Move on to the next node in ascending numerical order.
3. Identify all the activities that end on the node.
4. Calculate the EF time for each of these activities: this is given by the ES time of the activity plus its duration.
5. Then, the ES time for all the activities starting on the node under consideration is equal to the highest of the EF times calculated in step 4 above.
6. Repeat steps 2 to 5 until all nodes have been considered. If there are no more nodes to consider, the final node considered will be the end-of-project node.

Note that:

- Because all activities starting on a particular node have the same ES time, that ES time may be associated with the node.
- For those activities which end on the end-of-project node, the activity with the highest EF time (which is the ES time of the end-of-project node) is clearly the last activity to finish in the entire project. Therefore, this time defines the earliest possible completion time for the entire project.

Table 8.3 lists the ES and EF times for the activities in the EBSP Detector Project, calculated by the above method. These times are also shown in Figure 8.4, which is an enhanced version of the AOA diagram of Figure 8.3. The ES time of the end-of-project node is 26 days: the project should be completed after 26 working days.

The earliest start and finish times of the activities in the network only tell half the story. We are also interested in the latest times at which we can start activities, and the latest times at which they can finish, without jeopardizing the minimum project completion time we have found by considering earliest times. These are the *latest start* (LS) times and *latest finish* (LF) times for the activities. They are found by making a backward pass through the network (working through the nodes in *descending* numerical order), carrying out the following operations:

Table 8.3 ES, LS, EF and LF times, total and free slack, and critical path status for the activities of the EBSP Detector Project

Activity	ES time (day)	LS time (day)	EF time (day)	LF time (day)	Total slack (days)	Free slack (days)	Critical?
D1	0	0	1	1	0	0	YES
D2	1	6	2	7	5	5	NO
D3	1	1	2	2	0	0	YES
D4	2	2	7	7	0	0	YES
D5	7	7	13	13	0	0	YES
C1	13	14	18	19	1	0	NO
C2	13	13	23	23	0	0	YES
C3	18	19	22	23	1	1	NO
C4	13	16	21	24	3	3	NO
C5	23	23	24	24	0	0	YES
C6	24	24	25	25	0	0	YES
C7	25	25	26	26	0	0	YES

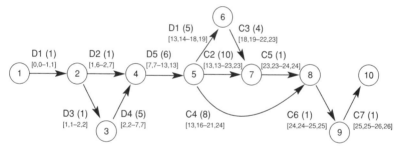

Figure 8.4 An activity-on-arrow (AOA) diagram for the EBSP Detector Project

1. Starting at the end-of-project node, assign all activities that end on this node an LF time equal to the earliest project completion time (that is, the ES time for the end-of-project node).
2. Move on to the next node in descending numerical order.
3. Identify all the activities that start on the node.
4. Calculate the LS time for each of these activities: this is given by the LF time of the activity minus its duration.
5. Then, the LF time for all the activities finishing on the node under consideration is equal to the lowest of the LS times calculated in step 4 above.

6. Repeat steps 2 to 5 until all nodes have been considered. If there are no more nodes to consider, the final node considered will be the start-of-project node.

Note that, because all activities finishing on a particular node have the same LF time, that LF time may be associated with the node.

Table 8.3 lists the LS and LF times for the activities in the EBSP Detector Project, and they are also shown in Figure 8.4.

8.2.6 Critical path

In a project, there will generally be some activities which can be delayed to some degree without jeopardizing the completion time of the project, while for others, no such leeway exists. In a critical path analysis, activities which cannot be delayed can be recognized because their ES times and LS times will be the same. Any activity for which the ES and LS times (or EF and LF times) are the same are said to be *critical*. Any delay in such an activity will delay completion of the entire project. In the EBSP Detector Project, D1, D3, D4, D5, C2, C5, C6 and C7 are critical, as comparison of the ES and LS (or EF and LF) columns in Table 8.4 indicates. Together, these activities make up a *critical path* through the project: a sequence of activities which must be completed on schedule if the project is to be completed at the earliest possible time.

Non-critical activities have *slack*: delays to them, within limits, should not affect the completion of the project. In the EBSP Detector Project, the amount of slack associated with non-critical activities may be determined by inspection of Figure 8.4. Slack is often described in terms of:

- *Total slack:* the amount of slack available to an activity in total.
- *Free slack:* the amount of slack available to an activity without impinging on the slack of any subsequent activity.

The total slack and free slack associated with the activities of the EBSP Detector Project are listed in Table 8.4. These slacks may be derived from the diagram Figure 8.4.

8.2.7 Dummy activities

In practice, constructing an AOA network can be complicated by two factors.

The first problem is that, by convention, no two activities should start and end on the same pair of nodes. This is because in some versions of CPM, activities are identified solely by their start and end nodes, so activities starting and ending on the same pair of nodes would be confused. Therefore, where two activities span the same pair of nodes, a *dummy* activity is inserted into the network. Such a dummy activity, since it does not correspond to a real activity, has a duration of 0, and consumes no resources. Conventionally, to resolve the problem of two activities spanning the same pair of nodes, the dummy activity is inserted in series with the activity of shorter duration, following the activity. Figure 8.5 illustrates how this works. If more than two activities span the same pair of nodes, additional dummy activities must be inserted, as appropriate.

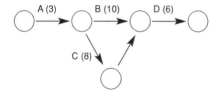

Figure 8.3 A dummy activity is used to distinguish between activities B and C, which would otherwise start and end on the same pair of nodes

The second problem can arise when two or more activities require different combinations of particular activities to be completed before they can be started. Under these circumstances, the logic of the precedence relationships cannot be represented by the CPM technique as described so far. This kind of problem may be solved by judicious use of one or more dummy activities. Figure 8.6 gives an example of a dummy activity used in this way.

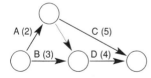

Figure 8.6 Activity D must be preceded by both of activities A and B, but activity C need only be preceded by activity A: to represent this logic, a dummy activity is required

8.2.8 CPM: concluding comments

The critical path method provides a means of assembling information on project activity precedence relationships and durations in a form which allows the user to:

- Calculate earliest and latest start and finish times for all the activities.
- Calculate the minimum duration of the entire project from start to finish.
- Identify the critical activities in the project.
- Calculate the total slack and the free slack associated with the non-critical activities.

The activity-on-arrow diagram is central to manual use of the technique. Although the principles underlying the construction of AOA diagrams are straightforward, drawing large networks without automated aid is both time-consuming and difficult, and is, therefore, not recommended. Fortunately, modern software, such as that discussed in Chapter 9, can handle the logic of such networks routinely. Note, however, that several software packages do not include visual display of AOA diagrams, though they generally provide the quantitative information which would be generated by such diagrams.

8.3 The Gantt chart

A highly valued mode of displaying projects, supported by most software packages, is the *Gantt chart* (also sometimes known as the *schedule graph*). The Gantt chart is closely related to the AOA diagram, of which it can be regarded as a specialized form.

A Gantt chart displays the component activities of a project as horizontal lines (or bars or arrows) in a sequence corresponding to their schedule. The length of the line representing an activity is proportional to the duration of the activity, and the horizontal axis of the chart can be interpreted as a calendar. Activities are distinguished from each other by displaying them at different heights on the graph. Figure 8.7 displays the EBSP Detector Project in Gantt chart form. In this Gantt chart, critical activities are highlighted with bold lines, and broken lines indicate the slack associated with non-critical activities.

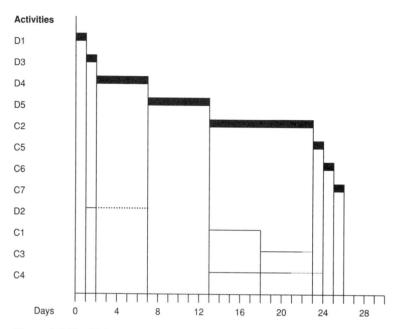

Figure 8.7 The EBSP Detector Project displayed as a Gantt chart

The major advantage of a Gantt chart is that it provides an easily interpreted graphical representation of the sequence and durations of the component activities of a project, and the availability of slack time within the project. It is probably the most comprehensible all-round representation of a project schedule, and it can be a valuable aid in enabling managers, generally, to understand and appreciate the structures of their projects, and, specifically, to schedule activities in order to use resources effectively. However, the precedence relationships between activities are not as clearly identified as in an AOA diagram.

The Gantt chart was in use as a planning tool many decades before the development of critical path methods. It does not in itself offer any analysis beyond what can be done by eye, and it is probably for this reason that many formal treatments of critical path methods apparently disdain it, and mention it only in passing, if at all. Yet, its immediacy as a comprehensible picture of a project is undeniable. It is probably of most value when used to picture a relatively small number of activities together (perhaps no more than 100, and maybe substantially less). It can be particularly helpful, therefore, in enabling managers to view projects in their entirety, composed of a relatively small number of fairly aggregate activities at high hierarchical levels on a work breakdown structure.

To draw a Gantt chart, it is most straightforward to graph the critical activities first, and then add the non-critical activities. Therefore, for all but the most simple projects, it is useful to have carried out a critical path analysis with an AOA diagram first.

8.4 Introducing duration uncertainty into network schedules

The CPM analysis in Section 8.2 assumed that all activity durations were known with certainty. However, in practice it is frequently appropriate to include explicit recognition of uncertainty in specifying activity durations in the construction of a network schedule. The standard approach to this is often referred to as the *project evaluation and review technique* (PERT). Much of PERT analysis is identical to that of CPM. However, there are some vital differences.

In the PERT approach, duration uncertainty is introduced by inviting the user to specify just three parameters for each activity: a *most likely duration* (m), an *optimistic shortest feasible duration* (a), and a *pessimistic longest feasible duration* (b). These three parameters, it is reckoned, are fairly easy to conceptualize, although, of course, that does not mean that they are easy to actually specify!

Making some assumptions about the nature of duration uncertainty in projects, the three parameters can be used to specify a *probability distribution* for each activity: that is, a mathematical function that indicates the likelihood or probability that the duration of an activity will fall between any two durations the user cares to name. The particular probability distribution that is generally used in PERT is the *Beta probability distribution*. Moder *et al.* (1983) note that the Beta distribution 'has the desirable properties of being contained inside a finite interval, and can be symmetric or skew, depending on the location of the mode, m, relative to a and b'. However, they note that use of the Beta distribution in this context is 'lacking an empirical basis' (p. 283). It is generally recognized that use of the Beta distribution in PERT has a lot to do with convenience, and rather less to do with any strong indication that it is particularly appropriate to the specification of project activity durations. Figure 8.8 illustrates some Beta probability distributions for three different activities specified by three sets of parameters a, b and m. Note that these three activities all happen to have the same most likely estimated duration (m), and differ only in the optimistic and pessimistic duration estimates (a and b). Note how the different relative values of a, b and m produce differently shaped probability distributions.

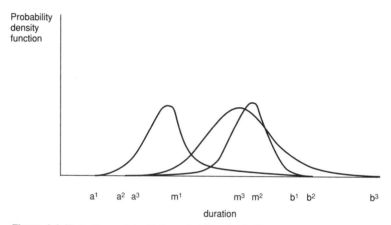

Figure 8.8 Illustrations of the Beta probability distribution

In order to use the PERT estimates of activity durations within a critical path network analysis, it is useful to specify two further parameters of each activity duration that can be calculated from the a, b and m estimates. One of these parameters is an 'average' duration, and the other is a measure of the degree of uncertainty, or 'spread' of the probability distribution.

To specify the average duration of an activity, its *mean*, or *expected value*, is calculated. The mean can be understood as a weighted average, averaging all the values that the duration can take, but weighting them according to their likelihood. Generally, the mean differs from the most likely value (when the probability distribution is symmetric, then the mean and most likely values are the same). To calculate the mean of a Beta distribution precisely requires a complex formula. In PERT calculations, it is almost universal practice to use a very simple, but good, approximation for the mean, μ:

$$\mu = (a + 4m + b)/6$$

The spread of the distribution is described by the *standard deviation*. Generally, under particular assumptions, about 68 per cent of the distribution is expected to lie within one standard deviation of the mean, about 95 per cent within two standard deviations, and over 99 per cent within three standard deviations. For the Beta distribution, the standard deviation, σ, is calculated, once again, by a simple but good approximation:

$$\sigma = (b - a)/6$$

Another measure of spread that is used is the *variance*, σ^2, which is simply the square of the standard deviation:

$$\sigma^2 = ((b - a)/6)^2$$

To recapitulate the argument so far: to explicitly include uncertainty in critical path analysis, the user needs to specify the duration uncertainty for each activity in terms of three estimates (most likely, optimistic and pessimistic) of duration. These estimates may then be used in the formulae above to calculate the mean, the standard deviation, and the variance for the duration of each activity.

In the basic CPM approach described in Section 8.2, with each activity was associated just one, certain, measure of duration. Now we have a situation in which there are six parameters associated with the duration of each activity: the three input estimates, and the mean, standard deviation, and variance.

To analyse the project further, the mean values of the activity durations can be used in place of the certain durations in order to carry out a critical path analysis. The underlying rationale for this is that mean durations can be manipulated as though they were certain durations. If, for example, you have a set of activities carried out one after the other, in series, then the mean duration of the entire series of activities is the sum of the means of the component activities. Actually, this is only true if the probability distributions of the component activities are *statistically independent*: that is, the actual value of any particular activity is not influenced by the actual value of any of the other activities. This might seem a reasonable assumption. Actually, it is quite restrictive. Nevertheless, we shall assume it for now.

In particular, the above method for handling mean durations implies that the mean duration of the critical path, and therefore the project, is simply the sum of the mean durations of the critical activities.

Generally, the variance of the project duration is generally taken to be the sum of the variances of the activities on the critical path. Note that the standard deviation of the overall duration is not the sum of the standard deviations of the critical path activities. If you want to know the standard deviation of the project duration, as well you might, you need to calculate its variance, and then find the square root of the variance.

Strictly, the above method of calculating the variance of the duration of a project only calculates the variance of the critical path. It assumes that no matter what the actual durations of the activities turn out to be, the critical activities will remain critical: it takes no account of the possibility that, under uncertainty, other paths might turn out to be critical instead. Thus, it is generally reckoned that estimating the variance (and, by implication, the standard deviation) of a project in this way can lead to underestimates of the variance by up to the order of 25 per cent.

Table 8.4 provides a reworking of duration estimates for the EBSP Detector Project, in which the technician has tried to represent her uncertainty about the duration of various activities in terms of the

Table 8.4 Most likely, optimistic and pessimistic duration estimates for the activities of the EBSP Detector Project, and the corresponding calculated mean, standard deviation and variance values

Activity	Most likely duration (days)	Optimistic duration (days)	Pessimistic duration (days)	Mean (days)	Standard deviation (days)	Variance (days²)
	m	a	b	m	σ	σ^2
D1	1	1	1	1.00	0.00	0.00
D2	1	1	2	1.17	0.17	0.03
D3	1	1	2	1.17	0.17	0.03
D4	5	3	10	5.50	1.17	1.36
D5	6	4	12	6.67	1.33	1.78
C1	5	4	15	6.50	1.83	3.36
C2	10	5	15	10.00	1.67	2.78
C3	4	3	6	4.17	0.50	0.25
C4	8	5	9	7.67	0.67	0.44
C5	1	1	3	1.33	0.33	0.11
C6	1	1	1	1.00	0.00	0.00
C7	1	1	2	1.17	0.17	0.03

three PERT estimates: most likely (*m*), optimistic (*a*), and pessimistic (*b*). The table also shows the mean, standard deviation, and variance of each activity, as calculated by the formulae given above.

The expected durations provided in Table 8.4 form the basis for a revised activity-on-arrow diagram for the project. This is shown in Figure 8.9. As in the case of certainty, ES, LS, EF and LF times have been calculated. The results of these calculations are listed in Table 8.5. Comparing Table 8.5 with Table 8.3 (for the project with the original, certain, duration data) we can see that activity C2 has ceased to be critical, while activities C1 and C3 have become critical. On the basis of the revised data, the estimated critical path through the network has changed. Summing the expected durations and variances of the critical activities, the mean duration of the entire project is found to be 28.50 days, and the variance is estimated at 6.92 days^2. This implies a standard deviation of 2.63 days.

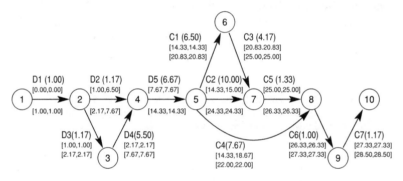

Figure 8.9 Activity-on-arrow diagram for the EBSP Detector Project, with revised data

Provided there are a reasonable number of activities on the critical path, and there is no reason to believe that there is any systematic skewness in the individual duration distributions, the probability distribution of the overall project duration can be regarded as being of a particular type: the *Normal* distribution, characterized by a bell-shaped probability distribution curve.

The Normal distribution has some useful properties. For a Normal distribution, 50 per cent of the distribution lies below the mean (and 50 per cent above, of course), 68 per cent of the distribution lies within one standard deviation of the mean, 95 per cent within two standard deviations, and over 99 per cent within three standard deviations, and the distribution is symmetric. Strictly, the EBSP Detector Project is composed of too few activities to safely regard its duration probability distribution as Normal, but, by way of example, the information in Table 8.6 has been derived (see also Figure 8.10).

Table 8.6 Probabilities of completion by various dates for the EBSP Detector Project.

Number of days into project	Number of standard deviations (2.63 days) from mean (28.50 days)	Probability of completion by this date
20.61	−3	0.0005
23.24	−2	0.0105
25.87	−1	0.16
28.50	0	0.5
31.13	+1	0.84
33.76	+2	0.9885
36.39	+3	0.9995

Because the Normal distribution is a standard shape, further information can be gleaned by reference to tables which provide details of the probabilities of values occurring in any given range. These tables are generally compiled for the *standard* Normal distribution with mean 0 and standard deviation 1. A simple arithmetic transformation allows any other normal distribution to be

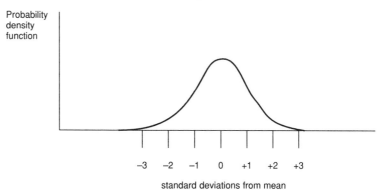

Probability density function

standard deviations from mean

Figure 8.10 The Normal probability distribution

interpreted in terms of the standard Normal distribution. In particular, it is possible to estimate the probability of completion by a particular number of days into the project, or the number of days into the project by which there is a particular probability of completion.

8.5 Trading-off duration and cost

It is frequently the case that the durations of particular activities in a project are not fixed, but can be varied. Other things being equal, it is generally sensible to attempt to reduce activities to their minimum durations, but, of course, other things are rarely equal. In particular, it can be the case that reduced duration of an activity may be bought at the expense of increased cost.

Consider once again the EBSP Detector Project example, and, for the sake of simplicity, assume that the original, non-probabilistic, duration estimates presented in Section 8.2 are valid (rather than the probabilistic estimates introduced in Section 8.4). Now, suppose that the durations of activities C1, C2, C3, and C4 as indicated in Table 8.1 are their 'normal' durations, and that, by incurring additional expense, the technician reckons that she can make them shorter. The more expense incurred, the shorter can these activities be, down to some limit known as the *'crash'* duration. Table 8.7 indicates, for each of these activities, the normal duration (that originally stated in Table 8.1), the crash duration (the shortest time to which the duration may be reduced) and the cost of duration reduction (expressed in cost incurred per day saved).

Table 8.7 Normal and crash durations, and costs of duration reductions, for activities C1, C2, C3 and C4 in the EBSP Detector Project.

Activity	Normal duration (days)	Crash duration (days)	Cost of reduction (£ per day)
C1	5	4	100
C2	10	5	200
C3	4	2	400
C4	8	5	100

Reducing the duration of component activities of a project may be worthwhile if it leads to a reduction in the overall project duration. Exploring the possibility of reducing project duration is best done by reference to the project Gantt chart (Figure 8.7). There is no point in reducing the duration of any activity unless it is on the critical path, because reducing the duration of non-critical activities will not affect the overall project duration.

For the EBSP Detector Project, reducing C2, on the critical path, by one day costs £200, and reduces the project duration by one day. It also results in a network in which the critical path splits into two: in addition to C2 being critical, so now are C1 and C3. This means that any further reduction in duration will have to involve both branches simultaneously. Figure 8.11 shows a revised Gantt chart depicting the new situation.

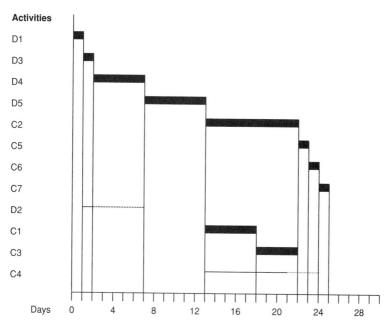

Figure 8.11 The Gantt chart of Figure 2.7, with activity C2 reduced by one day

To make a further reduction in project duration, either C1 and C2 together will have to be reduced, or C2 and C3 together. Reducing C1 and C2 together is cheaper than reducing C2 and C3 together, so the technician chooses to reduce the cheaper C1 and C2 combination. Reducing both of C1 and C2 by one day costs £300, and shortens the project by a further day. C1 is now at its lowest, crash, limit, of four days: therefore the further reduction must be of C2 and

C3 in combination. Reducing both of C2 and C3 by one day costs £600, and shortens the project by another day. Now C4 becomes critical: there are three branches to the critical path, and any further reduction in duration must involve all of C2, C3 and C4 together.

Reducing all of C2, C3 and C4 by one day each costs £700, and reduces the project duration by yet another day. We have now reached the crash duration limit for C3, and this means that no further reductions in project duration can be made. This *minimum time schedule* is shown in Figure 8.12, and the activity reductions that have been carried out to derive it are summarized in Table 8.8.

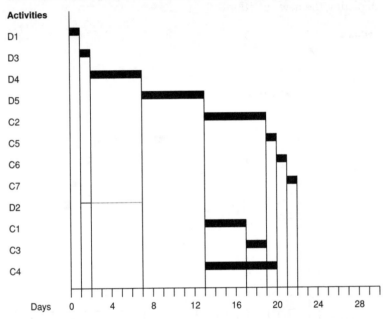

Figure 8.12 A minimum time schedule Gantt chart for the EBSP Detector Project

Table 8.8. Activity reductions to derive a minimum time schedule for the EBSP Detector Project

Step	Shortened activities	Cost (£)	Cumulative cost (£)	Days saved (cumulative)
1	C2, by 1 day	200	200	1
2	C1 & C2, each by 1 day	300	500	2
3	C2 & C3, each by 1 day	600	1,100	3
4	C2, C3 & C4, each by 1 day	700	1,800	4

The minimum duration schedule for the project is four days shorter than the original schedule, but has incurred an additional cost of £1800. In practice, there might be some compromise schedule that would be preferable to either extreme. For example, if an early completion bonus for the project of £400 per day were on offer, it would make sense to implement the first two duration reductions, but not the second two.

8.6 Resource usage

A particular strength of critical path network techniques for project planning is their use in aiding resource planning and in monitoring the usage of resources. In early implementations of critical path network techniques, such consideration of resources tended to be a 'luxury' add-on to the basic scheduling process. These days, it is perhaps the most important and valued feature of the approach. In the following subsections, we consider various aspects of both resource planning and the monitoring of resource usage.

8.6.1 Resource levelling

Consider once again the original EBSP Detector Project, as depicted in the Gantt chart of Figure 8.7. Fabrication of the mounting (C3), fabrication of the interface (C4), the construction of sub-assembly (C5) and construction of the final assembly (C6) all require the use of welding equipment. The welding equipment available to the laboratory is a scarce resource, in continual service for a variety of purposes, and there are strong pressures to minimize its daily use on the EBSP Detector Project. The Gantt chart indicates some possible difficulties in this respect. Employing an earliest-time schedule (in which all activities are started and finished at their earliest possible times), as depicted in Figure 8.7, would lead to activities C3 and C4 running in parallel for three days. Available slack might be exploited, however, to delay activity C3, which would allow the overlap to be reduced to two days, and therefore ease some of the pressure on the welding resource.

The above procedure is a simple example of *resource levelling*, in which the aim is to obtain as even a distribution of resource usage over time as possible, without delaying the final completion time of the project. Of course, there may be situations in which a manager judges it worthwhile to delay a project to some extent in order to obtain a more level resource usage profile. Indeed, fixed constraints on resources may make delays inevitable: under such *constrained-resource* conditions, the aim is to obtain the shortest possible project completion time, without violating resource constraints.

Suppose, for example, that in the EBSP Detector Project, employment of the welding resource were absolutely limited to usage on one activity per day. It would then be necessary to reschedule the project, since no activities which make use of the resource could run in parallel. A minimum time schedule under these conditions would be one in which C3 were delayed until the completion of C4, delaying the completion of the project by two days. It is important to recognise that this delay is caused by resource constraints, not precedence constraints: C3 could precede C4, but the project duration would be far greater.

Simple scheduling problems of the kind described above can be tackled by hand with the aid of a Gantt chart. However, for complex networks, with not just one but several resources to consider simultaneously, computer support is probably necessary. Most commercial software offers such support, although the number and type of resources that can be handled vary from package to package (see Maroto and Tormos 1994).

For complex resource scheduling problems, even with the assistance of software, it is unlikely that the best solution (for example, the shortest and most level schedule) will, in practice, be identified. There is, firstly, the problem of defining what a term such as 'most level' might, precisely, mean. More significantly, most commercial software packages use heuristic, rather than optimizing, resource scheduling algorithms. Different packages use different algorithms. Maroto and Tormos (1994) note that the details of the algorithms used are not usually supplied, and that different packages perform differently, with no package clearly performing best under all conditions.

8.6.2 Resource delaying

Monitoring the consumption of resources as a project proceeds may be as important as, or even more important than, monitoring the actual execution of the project over time. Suppose, for example, that each activity in the EBSP Detector Project is expected to consume the labour time of the technician at the cost rate of £100 per day.

(This is an unusually straightforward situation; normally, we would expect different activities to consume a resource at different rates.) From Table 8.1, the project should have a total labour cost of £4400 (since the total duration of all activities is 44 days). How this quantity is consumed over the duration of the project depends on the precise schedule adopted. Adopting the earliest time schedule of Figure 8.7 means that money will be spent sooner rather than later.

As a general rule, it is better to spend money later rather than sooner, other things being equal. This heuristic is often formally expressed by discounting the value of money, in proportion of the length of time into the future when it is to be spent, to its *net present value* (NPV). If this kind of criterion is important in the EBSP Detector Project, then a schedule should be adopted which delays activities until their latest possible times. Figure 8.13 shows such a *latest time schedule*. This schedule will delay costs until the latest possible time, but its disadvantage is that a delay to any of the activities could delay the entire project. Table 8.9 compares the labour cost profiles of earliest time and latest time schedules for the EBSP Detector Project.

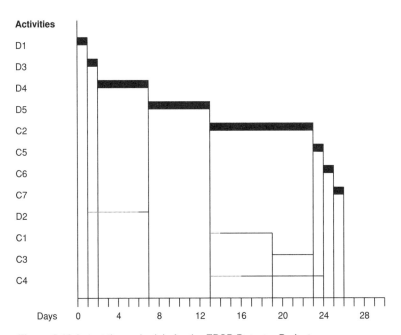

Figure 8.13 Latest time schedule for the EBSP Detector Project

Table 8.9 Cost profiles for earliest time (ET) and latest time (LT) schedules for the EBSP Detector Project

Day	Earliest time schedule: expenditure (£)	Earliest time schedule: cumulative expenditure (£)	Latest time schedule expenditure (£)	Latest time schedule expenditure (£)
1	100	100	100	100
2	200	300	100	200
3	100	400	100	300
4	100	500	100	400
5	100	600	100	500
6	100	700	100	600
7	100	800	200	800
8	100	900	100	900
9	100	1000	100	1000
10	100	1100	100	1100
11	100	1200	100	1200
12	100	1300	100	1300
13	100	1400	100	1400
14	300	1700	100	1500
15	300	2000	200	1700
16	300	2300	200	1900
17	300	2600	300	2200
18	300	2900	300	2500
19	300	3200	300	2800
20	300	3500	300	3100
21	300	3800	300	3400
22	200	4000	300	3700
23	100	4100	300	4000
24	100	4200	200	4200
25	100	4300	100	4300
26	100	4400	100	4400

2.6.3 Monitoring of resource usage

Suppose the earliest time schedule of Figure 2.7 is adopted for the EBSP Detector Project, and the technician responsible for the project decides to check progress at the end of the seventh, thirteenth and eighteenth days of the project, when particular activities are scheduled to end. On the first two progress checks, we may suppose that all is as scheduled. By the end of day 18 of the project (the date of the third progress check), the Gantt chart of Figure 8.7 indicates that C1 should be complete, C2 should be half completed, and C4 should be two-fifths completed. Further, Table 8.9 indicates that £2900 should have been expended in labour costs to date.

Suppose, however, that the third progress check, at the end of day 18, reveals that, in fact, while C1 and C4 are on schedule, C2 is running about a day behind, while labour expenditure to date has been £3000. More detailed examination reveals that £100 extra has been spent in completing C1 on schedule. It also reveals that labour expenditure on C2 to date has been £500, which is what it should have been if it had been running to time: this indicates over-expenditure on C2, completion of which now appears likely to cost more than the £1000 originally budgeted.

The technician responsible for the project might note that late completion of C2, on the critical path, is threatening the completion date of the entire project, and that over-expenditure on both C1 and C2 indicates that the project budget is threatened too. Possible responses to these findings might include: actions to reduce the costs of subsequent activities; examination of activity C2 to ascertain whether it is being executed competently; re-estimation of the durations and the costs of subsequent activities in the light of performance; or, acceptance of delay and additional costs as being within acceptable tolerance limits, or simply inevitable.

An observer might point out that the problems might have been detected sooner had progress of the project been monitored more frequently: daily, for example. This is possibly true. Clearly, there is a trade-off to be made between the degree of monitoring that takes place, and the costs that such monitoring incurs.

Critical Path Network Software

9.1 Introduction

Undoubtedly, much of the power of critical path network techniques is due to the fact that there exist powerful and reliable user-friendly implementations of the techniques for use on personal computers (PCs). Prior to the introduction of such implementations, it was virtually impossible, in many situations, for a manager to work interactively with a critical path network model: the available technology meant that critical path work was kept 'in the realm of minicomputers, if computers were used at all, and expert staff' (Gallagher 1997, p. 494). Computers were non-portable, so that even if one possessed the necessary expertise, there was little scope for their use in the field. Consequently, the simplest changes to a model might take hours, days, or even weeks to effect.

The radical developments in computer technology that have taken place since the early 1980s have transformed the situation. 'Now the PC is powerful enough and the software is easy enough to use that there are few business ventures that can't benefit from project management software' (Gallagher 1997, p. 494). Relatively naïve users can develop critical path models quickly, altering the models takes minutes or seconds, and the implications can be displayed immediately in graphical terms. All this can be done wherever one can take a PC. Consequently, the role of the critical path network model has changed from that of project 'icon' – an ideal image of the project, the detail of which may bear little resemblance to that of the actuality – to a working tool which, in reasonably skilled hands, can genuinely facilitate routine planning and monitoring at many different management levels. Stott (1998) comments: 'over the past few years, the project management software industry has gone through a major culture change as fundamental as the introduction of the first project management software back in the 1960s. Developments in computer hardware and user interfaces like Microsoft Windows have made the software available in the project management industry radically different from earlier generations of similar software' (p. 418).

This chapter considers the computer implementation of critical path network techniques. Most of the chapter focuses on commercially available software packages for carrying out critical path analysis and related activities on PCs, and considers the types of features that such packages offer. However, the chapter concludes with a section which briefly discusses the implementation of critical path network approaches on general spreadsheet software packages.

9.2 Commercial critical path network software

A multitude of critical path network software packages for the PC are commercially available. Among some of the most well-known packages at the time of writing are *MS Project* by Microsoft, *CA Superproject* by Computer Associates, and *Primavera Project Planner* and *Supertrak Project Manager* by Primavera. New packages are constantly being introduced, and old ones upgraded, so it is not easy to provide an up-to-the-minute review. Rather than attempting such a review, this section discusses the main features of critical path network software, and the issues involved with selecting and using it.

The costs of critical path network packages varies considerably. At the time of writing, prices range from a few hundred pounds sterling to a few thousand, the price tending to reflect the sophistication of the product. The cheaper end of the market includes a number of popular general-purpose packages which are adequate for use in managing many kinds of project. The more expensive packages tend to be appropriate for particularly large or complex projects. Most available software runs under Windows; some packages also have versions that run on other operating platforms. The requirements of most packages are well within the specifications of most contemporary PCs. Requirements for additional hardware are dependent upon the uses to which the software is to be put; possible requirements include high-quality colour printing, high-quality electronic display facilities, and electronic communication capability.

9.2.1 Ease of use

For most managers and other users, ease of use is an extremely important criterion when evaluating a software package. Reviewing critical path network software in 1995, Gallagher (1995) observes that there is a trade-off between the ease with which a user can learn to use a package, and the power of the package: 'an application that's easy to learn will get you up and running swiftly, but it may not be capable of the job that you need it for. Conversely, you may struggle with the most powerful systems simply because they are so powerful' (p. 349). However, the ubiquity of Windows as a platform for commercial software packages of this kind, and the consequent adoption of Windows operating conventions, has alleviated the problem of mastering powerful packages to quite an extent. Gallagher goes on to note that 'Windows may not be a total panacea, but today's project management software is more straightforward to use because it is Windows-based' (p. 349), and he recommends that 'when you have the option, only consider Windows-based software' (p. 354).

Understanding how to operate a package does not, in itself, enable the user to use it properly and effectively. It is also necessary to have a real appreciation of what the package does, and some prior understanding of the underlying theory of critical path approaches (such as this text provides) is valuable. It is not easy to pick up such an understanding of the approaches by simply learning to use the software. Maroto and Tormos (1994), reviewing a number of critical path network packages, comment: 'it is essential to have previous knowledge of scheduling techniques and project control for an appropriate use of these management packages. The documentation the packages provide, even those of the highest quality, does not make up for this fact' (p. 220).

To learn to use a critical path network scheduling package requires hands-on experience, and is greatly facilitated by a software tutorial and appropriate accompanying documentation. While most packages provide such material, the quality and thoroughness of it can vary considerably from package to package.

9.2.2 Graphical displays

As might be expected, graphical displays are central to modern critical path networks software, both as a means of presenting data, and as a mode of entering and manipulating data. Gallagher (1995) observes that though software that operates under DOS offers graphical displays 'you'll be better able to manipulate the graphical data under Windows' (p. 354). There seems little doubt that Gantt charts are the simplest types of visual display to understand and interpret, particularly for non-experts, though experts, too, often prefer them, and, according to Gallagher (1997), 'there's probably not a single project management package that can't display projects this way' (p. 495).

However, the amount of information Gantt charts can convey, particularly about interdependencies between activities, is limited. Stott (1998) notes that most software offers both displays based on Gantt charts and displays based on network diagrams (AOA or AON), which emphasize the relationships between activities. AON diagrams are more common than AOA diagrams. Maroto and Tormos (1994) observe that of the five leading packages they reviewed in 1994, only one then offered AOA diagramming, while Dawson and Dawson (1995) report that, in the mid-1990s, 'project management software tools are moving away from activity-on-the-arrow representations towards activity-on-the-node representations', with a general movement 'towards standardised activity-on-the-node and Gantt chart Windows products' (p. 354). Whether or not this trend is regrettable is debatable; while AOA diagrams are an extremely convenient basis for *manual* critical path network calculations, use of a computer obviates the need for such manual calculations for all intents and purposes. Under these circumstances most users would probably find it easier to work with AON diagrams than AOA diagrams, particularly when specifying or examining logical inter-relationships between activities. This is certainly the view of Dawson and Dawson (1998), who consider AOA diagrams to be 'less intuitive' than AON diagrams.

9.2.3 Resource scheduling

Relating usage of resources to activities in a project is one of the most useful features of critical path network software tools. Most packages permit at least several hundred different resources to be considered, and therefore resource planning can be fairly detailed. Resources may include money, different types of materials, machine capacity, and skilled labour of various types. A particular instance of the latter is the case where individuals are represented as resources. Typically, resources are constrained and have costs associated with their use. Software will indicate whether or not a schedule violates constraints, and its implications for cost over the duration of the project.

Most software packages include facilities to automatically reschedule projects in order to avoid the violation of resource constraints, or, if this is impossible, to minimize them. Related to this is the facility to level resource usage: to make its usage rate over the duration of the project as constant as possible. Maroto and Tormos (1994) distinguish between *partial* resource levelling, in which the duration of the project is not increased, and resources are levelled within this constraint, so that the possibility of overload exists, and *full* resource levelling, where the duration of the project is allowed to increase to eliminate any overload.

Automatic resource scheduling and levelling is extremely valuable. The ability to actively assist managers in scheduling projects subject to the constraints imposed by the availabilities of various resources is central to the power and utility of modern software. The facility to be able to quickly and easily explore the implications of different resource availabilities, in terms of durations and costs, is highly valued by users. However, the facility must be used wisely: Stott (1998), for example, cautions that 'it is important to understand the rules used by a particular package when it performs such automatic scheduling or rescheduling of a project as it might not work in exactly the way you want it to' (pp. 419–20). Resource scheduling in critical path network software is carried out by means of heuristics: sets of rules which usually provide a good solution, but probably will not provide the very best solution, and may occasionally provide a poor solution. Such heuristics are used because there is no known practical optimization approach. Different packages use different heuristics, which vary in their characteristics and degree of sophistication. Maroto and Tormos (1994) noted that, when scheduling with limited resources (that is, trying to find a minimum duration schedule subject to constraints on resource usage), 'great differences' in results were obtained with different packages, 'which increased as the conflicts and the number of resources became larger' (p. 220). Maroto and Tormos observed that details of the heuristics used were not generally supplied with the packages they reviewed, echoing a similar complaint from Wasil and Assad

(1988), that 'software documentation is often cryptic about the levelling algorithm employed' (p. 81).

9.2.4 Communication and software compatibility

Traditionally in project management, a single individual, or set of individuals, might have access to the software model of a project. This may still be the case for modestly-sized projects, but for large projects, it is likely that many users will have access to it for a variety of purposes. These individuals may wish to access the model from different locations, possibly widely dispersed. Managers responsible for particular project segments may wish to consult the parts of the model relating to their responsibilities, or indeed update these parts. At higher levels, managers may seek more global views of the project and its progress. In a very real sense, the computer-based model of the project may become a means whereby managers routinely communicate information on project progress to each other.

Such requirements, of course, have implications for the software. It must be able to support this kind of multi-user operation, with appropriate safeguards to ensure that the model is secure (that is, it cannot be illegitimately tampered with) and that its integrity is maintained (that is, changes made by one user to part of the model are conveyed as appropriate to other parts of the model). Compatibility with other software, so that project models can be shared in various ways, can be important. Kotamaki and Hameri (1998), for example, describe a large project involving participants from over 35 countries, in which 'as the underlying project is globally distributed, the natural medium to manage the information is the World Wide Web (WWW)' (p. 33), and so, when the scheduling system is implemented, 'it should contain a World Wide Web interface to make it accessible throughout the world' (p. 28).

Compatibility with other software applications is also valuable for using parts of the model in other contexts, such as the preparation of reports and similar. More generally, critical path network software needs to be compatible with more general project management software. (It is important to note that, while within the operational research domain, many authorities use the term *project management* as though it were synonymous with critical path scheduling methods, other professionals, and, in particular project managers, regard critical path scheduling as just one aspect of project management, and it is this latter perspective that this text supports.) Much software is these days designed with such compatibility in mind.

Many organizations simultaneously run several projects which are likely to compete for organizational resources. Software for use in these contexts needs to be able to accommodate several such projects, so that overall project programme managers can appreciate the competition and manage it appropriately.

Overall, the importance of critical path network software as a means by which managers communicate and gain common understanding of the project or projects under their management can barely be underestimated. This aspect of such software is likely to increase as sophisticated computer communication networks become a more common feature of the workplace. Stott (1998) believes that 'as local area network technology has stabilised and really come into its own we are beginning to see yet another phase in the need for project management systems... Project management is the ideal workgroup application ...' Stott envisages integration of project managers throughout an organization by means of electronic communication, but emphasizes that 'an organisation needs to consider each level of its structure separately. The expert users will still require high-end professional level software whereas "tactical" or occasional users will need something rather more simple. In addition, the executive level user will be looking for more of an executive information system' (p. 421).

9.2.5 Selecting software

A number of guides to buying software (for example: Gallagher 1995, 1997; Stott 1998) provide lists of the various software specifications. Such specifications tend to change rapidly, and, in any case, provide a very partial view of the true value of software. More subjective qualities, such as user-friendliness and appropriateness for particular applications are harder to report objectively or concisely, and tend not to be included in general guides. The serious buyer is advised to consult, if possible, more detailed literature from vendors, speak to other users of software, and sample demonstration versions or the like.

Authors of guides also tend to offer checklists of criteria and features to consider when buying software. These tend to contain useful advice. Summarizing this advice, it is recommended that buyers of critical path network software consider at least the following questions:

- *User-friendliness:* how easy is the package to use? How long does it take to learn to use it properly? Can a novice user work with it effectively without knowledge of its more sophisticated aspects?
- *Appropriateness to requirements:* is the package appropriate to the project (or projects) for which it is to be used? Is it sufficiently large to accommodate the project? Is it needlessly too large? Does it offer the particular facilities (for example, resource scheduling and levelling) that are required?
- *Graphical displays:* are the range and quality of the graphical displays sufficient? Are the displays easy to interpret?
- *Input:* is it straightforward to input data to the package? Is it quick and easy to get a preliminary model of a project up and running? Is it quick and easy to add or change data, and to experiment with 'what-if' models?
- *Technical:* is the package compatible with other software with which it will be required to communicate? Is after-sales service available? Are appropriate training courses offered?

9.3 Critical path network applications on spreadsheets

For projects of any appreciable size, the use of specialized software is strongly recommended. However, the possibility of implementing critical path techniques on standard spreadsheet models has been demonstrated. Baker (1996) describes a project to move a suite of health service laboratory computer programs from one computer to another. The laboratory managers needed to monitor progress of the project, and, given that the project was fairly small, chose to do this by means of a critical path network approach implemented on the *Lotus 123* spreadsheet package.

The project was broken down into twenty component activities. An AOA diagram was prepared. Each activity was allocated a line of the spreadsheet, and by reference, as necessary, to the AOA diagram, expressions for the earliest and latest start and finish times of each activity were formulated. From this information, Gantt charts could then be generated within the spreadsheet. A particular issue in the project was the number of computer terminals required as the project progressed: the number of terminals was therefore a resource. Initially a schedule was developed in which all activities began at their earliest start times. Then, by eye, the managers were able to develop alternative schedules which enabled resource usage to be smoothed in more desirable ways.

Baker explains that the managers in his case could use spreadsheets, but had no experience with specialized critical path network software, which was not, in any case, available. He concludes: 'the simple application ... took just a few hours to complete and was seen as a much better option than attempting an analysis by hand alone. Buying and learning to use special purpose software for such a simple one-off situation would not have been considered a realistic proposition'. In general, 'many managers from a wide variety of disciplines are experienced and competent spreadsheet users. With a little prompting from a management scientist specialist, a spreadsheet can provide them with a very quick and cheap alternative to buying and learning to use special purpose software' (p. 12).

Edwards and Finlay (1997) describe in detail how to use spreadsheets to carry out critical path network analysis. They contend that 'spreadsheets are highly suitable for small projects, although they are unable to display data and results in the standard project network diagram form. For larger projects it is essential to use specialised software' (p. 245). My personal view is that, although critical path analysis is workable on a spreadsheet, it has severe limitations and is very much a compromise approach. I would judge it inappropriate for managing even small projects unless the user is likely to need such support so infrequently that the purchase of specialized software is not a realistic option.

10 Practical Application

10.1 Introduction

Conventional wisdom has it that critical path methods were invented independently by two US organizations during the late 1950s: while E. I. Du Pont de Nemours were developing their *Critical Path Method* (CPM) to schedule large projects, the Special Projects Office of the US Navy developed their *Project Evaluation and Review Technique* (PERT) specifically for use on the Polaris ballistic missile development programme. However, related techniques had been around for some time before that. Gantt developed his eponymous chart approach in the USA in the 1910s, while the little-known *harmonygraph* developed by Adamiecki in the 1890s in Poland is clearly no less than an early method of representing graphically the same logic that AOA diagrams represent. Morris (1994) provides an account of the early developments in this area in his very readable book on the management of projects, which, unusually, takes a chronological approach to the topic.

As has been noted in Chapter 9, the way in which critical path analysis techniques are used has evolved considerably from its early days. This has been due not so much to any great advance in theory – there has been comparatively little fundamental advance – but to the phenomenal increase in the ease, availability, power and convenience of computing as provided by the PC, in contrast to the mainframe machines of the 1950s and 1960s. This chapter provides an outline of the current practicalities of using critical path network techniques.

There is a tendency among workers in the field of operational research and management science to regard critical path methods as synonymous with project management. This is most definitely not the case. *The Project Management Handbook*, edited by Cleland and King (1988) contains 38 chapters, only one of which (Moder 1988) addresses critical path networks directly. Other chapters cover such topics as appropriate organizational management structures, contractual issues, human resource management, and many more. Baker et al. (1988), in an empirical study of the factors which affect project success, claim that although critical path methods 'do contribute to project success ... the importance of PERT-CPM is far outweighed by a host of other factors' including 'work breakdown structures, life-cycle planning, systems engineering, configuration management, and status reports. The overuse of PERT-CPM systems was found to hamper success. It was the judicious use of PERT-CPM which was associated with success' (p. 906). The authors conclude: 'PERT and CPM are *not* the be-all and end-all of project management' (p. 916).

To regard critical path network techniques as the dominant feature of project management is unlikely to be a sound basis for working with project managers or becoming a successful project manager oneself. In contrast, what is essential is a real appreciation of how network approaches fit in with the other skills and activities that make up project management.

10.2 Critical path analysis and the life cycle of projects

In order to discuss the way in which critical path analysis is used by managers during projects, it is useful to have some description of what projects are, and, in particular, how they develop over time. Projects are frequently described in terms of the *project life-cycle*: the phases through which a project moves from its inception to its completion. Different authors adopt different life-cycle characterizations. It is usually fairly straightforward to resolve these different characterizations as being essentially different descriptions of recognizably the same phenomena, but real differences in project life cycles do exist, for example between projects in different domains. Adams and Barndt (1988) adopt a four-phase description of the project life cycle. Within each phase, particular activities take place. High-level scheduling takes place in the first, *conceptual*, phase. This is followed, in the second, *planning*, phase, by more detailed planning which may necessitate changes to the overall schedule developed in the first phase. During the third, *execution*, phase, the schedule is used to monitor the progress of the project, and the schedule is modified in the light of experience. The project is brought to a conclusion in the fourth, *termination*, phase.

Meredith and Mantel (1995) and Turner (1993) both present different four-phase descriptions of the project management life cycle, while Chapman and Ward (1997) show how the Adams and Barndt (1988) framework can be developed into an eight-stage description, each stage of which in turn is subdivided into a number of steps.

It would be misleading to attempt to generalize too much about the way in which successful projects are planned, and dangerous to attempt to be too prescriptive. However, some generalities seem appropriate. Early planning (for example, during the first phase in the Adams and Barndt life-cycle) should generally be at a fairly high-level: the project is decomposed into a relatively small number of high-level activities. This enables the project manager, or project management team, to develop a firm conception of the nature of the project. At this stage, it may be appropriate to map out the high-level activities using a network diagram. Such a diagram will contain only higher-level activities, will be fairly simple in structure, and the quantitative scheduling information it contains is likely to be tentative. Indeed, it may contain no quantitative data. Despite its obvious limitations, such a diagram may nevertheless be useful in facilitating understanding of the likely overall structure of the project.

Assuming the project is to proceed, more detailed planning (for example, during the second phase of the Adams and Barndt life-cycle) is likely to involve top-down decomposition of the high-level activities into successively greater levels of detail. Typically, this process of decomposition produces a work breakdown structure (WBS), a comprehensive and detailed hierarchical representation of the work that needs to be done in order to realize the project. The WBS can then be used to identify the low-level activities that constitute the input to a critical path scheduling model. The implications of the schedule which critical path planning produces can be interpreted at successively higher levels of the WBS. At its most basic, critical path network planning is a bottom-up activity: the precedence relationships, durations and resource requirements of component activities are integrated to produce an overall schedule. However, in practice, it is also used in top-down fashion: it indicates how resources need to be allocated, and how, more generally, the design of the project needs to be amended, in order to achieve top-level goals. This detailed planning, therefore, may result in considerable reconceptualization of the project, in order both to ensure that goals are met, or to reformulate goals which appear infeasible in the light of the detailed analysis.

Once execution of the project has commenced (for example, in the third and fourth phases of the Adams and Barndt life-cycle), the model is generally used both to monitor progress, by allowing comparison between scheduled progress and actual progress, and to explore and devise modifications to the project that become necessary as the project proceeds, often in response to deviations from the planned schedule.

10.3 The size and detail of projects

It is fairly evident that analysis of the kind that critical path methods provides is necessary in some form for the management of large projects involving many activities, resources and personnel. In the business climate of today, the use of software to carry out the analysis is virtually mandatory for any organization that wishes to have any hope of competing credibly, and the real issue is how its use should be integrated with the other functions of project management. For smaller projects, however, the use of critical path network software, and indeed the critical path approach itself, may be more questionable.

As far as the latter question is concerned, I am of the belief that virtually any project, no matter how small, can benefit from critical path analysis. Where such a project consists of only a handful of activities, and the stakes are low, such analysis may be pretty informal, and, indeed, non-explicit (that is, one might think it through, rather than committing it to paper, even on the proverbial back-of-an-envelope), but analysis in some appropriate form will be worthwhile.

The practicality of using critical path network techniques without computer assistance falls off rapidly with increasing number of project activities. For ten or twenty activities, manual techniques are feasible. Manual consideration of the structure of a relatively small number of strategic-level activities may precede more detailed, computer-aided, planning. Even for just a few activities, however, computations can be tedious and mistakes are easily made, particularly if the network structure is complex. Lock (1996) points out that even though it is perfectly feasible to carry out critical path analysis manually for a hundred or so activities, 'the biggest problem with any manual charting method … is that it is too inflexible. A change of plan to any except the very tiniest project can result in hours of tedious work in repositioning all the tasks on the chart. This is always coupled with the risk of introducing logical or other errors' (p. 220).

A more serious question is: how large does a project have to be before it is worthwhile investing in specialized software? (This question sets to one side the possibility, for small projects, of using a spreadsheet package for critical path analysis, as described in Chapter 9, which generally I do not recommend strongly.) Kidd (1991) cites the rule of thumb: 'if the network consists of 500 jobs or more, then a computer is needed to calculate the critical path; and if one has to undertake resource usage calculations this number falls to 150 tasks' (p. 139). A decade on, these numbers seem on the large side, and, indeed, Kidd goes on to remark that 'given the availability of microcomputer-based programs, it is unlikely that any network needs to be calculated by hand'. I would suggest that for any project consisting of 50 or more activities, the advantages of specialized software are indisputable, and that it is likely to contribute to the management of projects smaller than this, too. Wasil and Assad (1988), for example, cite a systems support firm which uses a microcomputer-based package 'to track the installation of new software on a mainframe computer on a daily basis. Its projects typically have 20 to 50 tasks and last two or three months' (p. 77).

Kayes (1995), describing his experience as a project manager in ICL during the 1970s, reports that he 'used a combination of PERT networks and bar (Gantt) charts to monitor the state of the project and resourcing needs. This was all done manually, largely because of the relatively small scale of the project, which involved no more than six ICL people over a two year project' (p. 325). He observes, though, that on a project of similar size in another organization, on which a computerized PERT system was used, 'the computer-produced output added credibility to … progress reports' (p. 325).

A related issue is how detailed the modelling of a project network should be. Shtub *et al.* (1994) recommend that the duration of activities in a project network should be in the range 0.5 per cent to 2 per cent of the project duration, but that activities that fall below this range should also be included, if they are critical. They also suggest that if the number of activities exceeds about 250, hierarchical structuring of the project into subprojects is essential.

Generally, hierarchical structuring has several advantages. For example, a particular activity may be the responsibility of a particular manager, who may find it useful to decompose the activity into a network of sub-activities in order to plan and manage it. However, this sub-network may be irrelevant to planning at a more strategic level, where only the overall duration, and, perhaps, resource usage, of the activity are of interest.

Lock (1996) argues that 'it is probably as well to avoid showing jobs as separate activities if their durations amount to only a very small fraction of the expected total time-scale, especially if they do not require resources' (p. 170). He continues: 'it can be argued sensibly that a network path should be broken to include a new activity whenever the action moves from one department or organisation to another' (p. 170). Further, the level of detail should be sufficient to allow assignment of costs to relevant activities: 'certain aspects of cost reporting and control will be impossible if sufficient attention to certain activities is not given when the network diagram is prepared' (p. 172).

Another related issue is that of the costs associated with carrying out analysis. Addressing this issue, Shtub *et al.* (1994) remark: 'the cost of applying critical path methods is sometimes used as a basis for criticism. However, the cost of applying PERT or CPM rarely exceeds 2 per cent of total project cost. Thus this added cost is generally outweighed by the savings from improved scheduling and reduced project time' (p. 354).

As observed in Chapter 8, analysis of the uncertainty of project duration using the standard PERT approach assumes that the uncertainties in the durations of the component activities of the project are independent. In practice, one can envisage all kinds of reasons why this might not be the case: for example, there might be systematic underestimation or overestimation of durations, or there might be delaying (or accelerating) influences affecting many of the activities in a similar fashion. Under these circumstances, PERT is likely to underestimate the overall uncertainty in the duration of the project. (This is in addition to the underestimation of uncertainty due to using only critical activities to calculate overall uncertainty, as alluded to in Chapter 8.) Unfortunately, accommodating statistical dependence complicates analysis, both from a mathematical point of view and from the point of view of estimating the degree of dependence. As far as the former point is concerned, if statistical dependence is likely to be a serious issue, then resort to an alternative approach, such as computer simulation, may be advisable. As far as estimation of dependence is concerned, an appropriate analytic strategy might be to carry out the analysis under varying assumptions concerning dependence (for example, an optimistic scenario, where uncertainties are independent, and a selection of more pessimistic scenarios, where various dependencies are incorporated).

10.4 Critical path network approaches within organizations

Organizations are complex entities. Each organization has its own unique culture, and, indeed, different parts of an organization will have their own sub-cultures. The way things are done within an organization will be unique to that organization. The way particular techniques are used will be unique. To introduce new techniques, or to change the way in which techniques are used successfully, is generally not an easy task. Critical path network techniques are no exception. In any case, as with any technique, there is no one best way of using critical path network techniques within organizations. Appropriate use of the techniques will be contingent on many factors, and the manager or management scientist attempting to implement them should take these factors fully into account.

Dane *et al.* (1979) compared 18 similar forestry organizations in a region of the USA. Although all the organizations had attempted to introduce network scheduling methods, the introduction was only deemed successful in four of the organizations. Likelihood of successful introduction seemed strongly related to the height in the organization of the individual making the introduction. (This result is very much in keeping with similar results concerning other techniques and practices.) The authors also found that 'an announced purpose which is broad and general improves the chance of successful introduction' and that 'attempting to schedule specific individuals was viewed as so undesirable (by the individuals so scheduled) that these applications were allowed to die' (p. 98).

Woolsey (1992) provides an entertaining example of how merely collecting data for a critical path analysis (in his case, the most likely, optimistic, and pessimistic activity duration estimates for a

PERT analysis) can change the way in which an organization considers and executes its operations.

It is appropriate to mention various extensions to the critical path analysis methods which have been developed and used at various times. GERT (Graphical Evaluation and Review Technique) accommodates, in particular, activities which have a *probability* of occurring rather than certainty (see Pritsker 1968). VERT (Venture Evaluation and Review Technique) accommodates multiple criteria in analysis rather than assigning priority to duration (see Kidd 1990). By and large, such approaches, in which analysis is carried out by computer simulation rather than by network analysis, have not been widely adopted.

Resource scheduling has been treated in this text as a refinement (albeit a fairly essential one) of the critical path approach. Gordon and Tulip (1997) present a historical outline of resource scheduling considered as an area in its own right.

There is a strong relationship between critical path analysis and project risk analysis. Indeed, at one time the two terms were considered virtually synonymous by many, though few would subscribe to this view now. Project risk analysis is a far more comprehensive activity than critical path analysis. It tends to focus on the 'big picture', and typically the networks upon which it would be framed would consist of relatively few 'high-level' activities. Critical path analysis would be expected to inform project risk analysis, however. For a thorough treatment of project risk analysis, see, for example, the book by Chapman and Ward (1997).

11 A Survey of Critical Path Methods Literature

11.1 Introduction

Critical path network analysis techniques are regarded as one of the 'classic' mathematical operational research topics, along with such other topics as linear programming, inventory modelling, and computer simulation. For this reason, introductory treatments are to be found, as a rule, in most general OR texts. However, they are not, and should not be regarded as, exclusive to OR, and similar introductory treatments can be found in general texts on operations management and project management, in particular. More specialized texts, dedicated to the topic, are also available, pitched at a range of categories of reader. Finally, the research literature abounds with papers describing both theoretical and practical developments in the area, as well as review articles and case studies.

11.2 Introductory material

Most general text books on operational research contain a chapter or so on critical path network analysis techniques, though there are some exceptions. These treatments are generally pitched at about the mathematical level of this book, though the chattiness varies considerably from book to book. The treatments generally focus on manual techniques for, in particular, developing and using both deterministic (CPM) and probabilistic (PERT) AOA diagrams. Anderson *et al.* (1994), Render and Stair (1994), and Waters (1989), for example, provide accounts that are particularly accessible to non-mathematical readers. By contrast, authors such as Taha (1987) and Winston (1994) tend to assume more mathematical sophistication in their readers.

Similar treatments can be found in introductory texts in other areas. Schroeder (1989) and Waters (1991), for example, include discussions of critical path approaches in their books on operations management techniques. In the more general management area, Targett (1996), for example, includes such a discussion, while Chapman *et al.* (1987) include a chapter on critical path methods within a book on management aimed specifically at engineering students. Van Gundy (1988) provides a sketchy account of the critical path approach in his book on structured problem-solving techniques.

General project management texts usually contain descriptions of critical path approaches. These treatments vary in depth according to the overall intentions of the texts. A point in favour of such treatments is that they tend to provide a balanced view of the importance of critical path approaches within project management, and frequently demonstrate how such approaches are integrated with other functions of project management. Meredith and Mantel (1995) and Turner (1993) provide a fairly concise and basic treatment. Lock (1996) provides a more extensive treatment, with attention to practicalities and computer usage. Moder (1988) provides a chapter on critical path methods in the *Project Management Handbook* edited by Cleland and King (1988). Lockyer and Gordon (1995) provide a two-part treatment, which first discusses project management in general, and then focuses on critical path network approaches.

11.3 Specialized texts

There are several specialized texts on critical path methods. Older texts were, of course, written before the advent of the PC, and consequently discuss the methods in a different kind of practical context from those experienced by most contemporary users. Nevertheless, many of these texts provide good introductions to the theory, and many of the practical issues they mention are still relevant today despite the change in context. For example, the books by Levin and Kirkpatrick (1966), Lowe (1969), and Lang (1977) provide treatments of theory at a similar level to this text, but in a more thorough manner. For an exploration of the more mathematical aspects of critical path methods, the well-respected text by Moder *et al.* (1983) is useful.

More recent texts provide a more contemporary context, though the rapid advance in the sophistication of PCs and critical path software makes it hard to be fully up-to-date. These more recent texts include those by Callahan *et al.* (1991), and O'Brien (1993), both of which emphasize the practical use of critical path approaches by project management within the construction industry; and Hutchings (1996), which is an advanced manual for project schedulers, also within the construction industry.

11.4 Case studies and other material

There are few case studies that simply describe the use of the critical path approach in a fairly contemporary context. Most such case studies of the approach date back to a time when computing was far less advanced, and practice was correspondingly different. Though up-to-date material does exist, it tends to describe, for research purposes, particular aspects of the approach rather than providing an overall picture. Much of this contemporary (at the time of writing) research material is discussed in Chapter 12.

Some earlier material can still be of interest, however. Schonberger (1981) uses a simple example to demonstrate that critical path analysis tends to underestimate overall project duration as a result of failing to take into account shifts in critical paths due to delays in non-critical activities (see Section 8.4). He observes that the conventional approach is 'to intensively manage critical path activities', but concludes that it makes more sense 'to intensively manage the most complex, delay-prone segments of the project network' (p. 69) in which many activities are scheduled in parallel and have highly uncertain durations. Interestingly, Schonberger is among the many authorities who do not feel that the three activity duration estimates of PERT offer much advantage in analysis over the single estimate of CPM, but recommends instead subjective re-evaluation of results based on an understanding of where delays are most likely to occur.

12 Current Issues in Critical Path Network Analysis

12.1 Introduction

This chapter concludes our discussion of critical path network techniques by reviewing recent and current research in the area.

Since their development in the 1950s, the rudiments of critical path methods, as described in standard texts, have remained much the same. The basics of the two independently developed AOA techniques, deterministic CPM and probabilistic PERT, have remained much as they started out. What has changed, however, is the way they are used. As the practice of project management has grown more sophisticated, and computers and their associated software have grown in power and accessibility, the role which critical path techniques plays within organizations has changed.

One might imagine, therefore, that current research in the field would be focused less on technical issues of critical path analysis, and more on the way in which such analysis fits into the wider practice of project management. This would reflect the growing general interest within management science on the *process* of using management science, rather than the techniques of management science itself. However, in actuality, reports on such research are fairly few.

One area of critical path techniques continues to attract research. The deficiency of standard PERT to correctly estimate the duration of a project has long been appreciated. This deficiency continues to attract new and ingenious approaches to improve such estimation.

12.2 Current issues in critical path methods use

The ubiquity of critical path methods makes the use of such methods standard for virtually any project of appreciable size that is to be formally managed, and many projects that are not.

However, the issue of how project managers use such methods is open, though the literature on the topic is disappointingly sparse. A problem that has attracted the attention of researchers in critical path analysis techniques is that of the underestimation of total project duration in PERT analysis, due to the feature of not taking account of the possibility of non-critical paths becoming critical that is characteristic of the approach. Computer-based Monte Carlo simulation has been used as an alternative approach. Various analytic techniques have also been proposed to improve upon the basic PERT technique. One of the most recent is the *back-forward uncertainty estimation* (BFUE) procedure suggested by Gong and Hugsted (1993). At the expense of additional calculation, this approach allows all paths through a network to be allowed for in calculation of overall duration. Gong and Hugsted claim that, compared with other such approaches, their approach has the additional advantage that it allows estimation of the effects of using up the float (or slack) of non-critical activities: 'until now, the slack-time use has been theoretically considered to be a safe area in project-time planning that can be used to adjust the start time of the noncritical-path activities without causing a delay in the total project time, although this is not true in some practical cases' (p. 166). Gong and Rowings (1995) develop this idea, introducing the notion of a safe range of float for an activity, related to the project managers' attitude to the risk of project duration delay. Gong (1997) provides an example of the BFUE approach in action, applied to a bridge construction project in which delaying a non-critical activity involving a hired tower crane implied, on the one hand, a lower rental charge, but, on the other, an increased risk of the activity becoming critical and causing additional costs due to penalty payments associated with overall project delay. The method facilitated an approach to trading-off the two effects.

Williams (1993) has observed that the standard notion of criticality is not always appropriate in PERT networks, because critical activities may pose very much less threat to overall project duration than other, non-critical, activities which may become critical due to probabilistic variation. As an alternative to the basic notion of criticality, Dodin and Elmaghraby (1985) have proposed an activity *criticality index*, which Williams interprets as an indication of the probability that the activity lies on the network critical path. Williams, however, favours an activity *cruciality index*, an indication of the strength of correlation between the duration of the activity and the duration of the entire project. Williams observes that 'it is often the case in studies that activities are found to have a high criticality but low cruciality, or low criticality and high cruciality. These activities need to be viewed in quite different ways. The former activities are known to be likely to be critical, so that it is worth management working at reducing their durations, or removing them from the critical path; however ... work to reduce their uncertainty would have little effect on the project outturn. The latter activities are quite different; they are unlikely to fall on the critical path, and so reducing the expected duration would have little effect; however, the high cruciality shows that, if they do become critical, their impact is very high ... so that effort must be applied to ensuring that the uncertainty is reduced. Obviously, activities whose criticality and cruciality indexes are both high warrant both types of attention' (p. 199).

Many other approaches to the general issue of assessing the uncertainty of overall project duration, and the contribution of individual activities to this uncertainty, have been explored. Cox (1995) provides a 'quick and simple' approach, based on a Normal approximation of activity duration uncertainties, which 'provides estimates which are superior to those obtained using the critical path approach' (p. 268). Kuklan *et al.* (1993) describe an enhanced PERT network which increases the attention given to non-critical activities. Cho and Yum (1997) define an uncertainty importance measure of an activity (UIMA). Mummolo (1994, 1997) has developed a PERT-path network technique (PPNT), which 'requires the same information as classical PERT-type network techniques do, but uses it more accurately' (Mummolo 1994, p. 89), and which compensates for the underestimation of traditional PERT analysis by considering 'all possible completion sequences of a project' (Mummolo 1997, p. 385). More radically, Jaafari (1996) argues that 'the trend to integrated risk management of construction projects requires a move away' (p. 298) from conventional network-based scheduling, and describes a time and priority allocation system (TAPAS) which, as part of an integrated project management information system (PMIS), constitutes such a move.

Williams (1995) questions whether the Beta distribution is appropriate to PERT analysis. He argues that in reality, there is often a very high probability that the central estimate of duration for an activity will be achieved or bettered, that such a central estimate often becomes a target duration, and that, consequently, work tends to slow down if an activity is proceeding faster than expected. He proposes an alternative modified triangular distribution for activity times which reflects his argument, and which, he claims, 'can be shown to reflect behaviour found in practice, and has indeed been used in the practical analysis of a large development project' (p. 1503).

Williams (1992) considers the choice of activity duration probability distributions for PERT analysis, questioning the standard choice of the Beta distribution, which 'is not easily understood, nor are its parameters easily estimated' (p. 268). Williams considers that in selecting a distribution, 'the parameters and distributions used must be meaningful to the project planner", and 'thus the problems of selecting a distribution and estimating its parameters are psychological and practical rather than mathematical' (p. 269). He favours a triangular distribution, and considers that points of 10 per cent and 90 per cent likelihood (probable minimum and maximum) are easier to estimate than absolute extremes.' He also suggests that where the uncertain durations of two or more activities have some degree of dependence, such 'correlation effects can be modelled using separate independent and common-cause elements' (p. 269).

The issue of diagramming has been considered by some researchers. Dawson and Dawson (1998) consider that AOA diagrams are 'less intuitive' than AON diagrams which they observe to be 'more common' (p. 299). They advocate the extension of standard AON diagrams to include probabilistic paths (to represent activities which may or may not occur) and probabilistic loops (to represent activities which may need to be repeated). They argue that if such extensions were available for popular software packages, the use of such packages to consider risk and uncertainty within projects would be enhanced. Although the same authors have considered similar generalization of AOA diagrams (Dawson and Dawson 1994), they clearly favour the development of AON diagrams (Dawson and Dawson 1995).

Alternative principles to those underlying conventional critical path analysis have been explored. Shtub (1992) describes an experiment, conducted in the form of a computer simulation, to compare the value of a critical path analysis approach to project control with an approach based on the *earned value* (EV) method. The progress of a project was modelled. Based on monitoring of the progress in comparison with the initial schedule, alterations were made to the project plan: in particular, more workers might be hired to improve progress. Whereas the critical path approach was based on monitoring the completion of activities, the EV approach was based on monitoring the value of work carried out. Shtub's results indicated that when uncertainty in estimating the work content is high, then the EV approach is superior to the standard critical path approach, but when the uncertainty is low, the converse is the case. He concludes that 'for any project performed under a tight schedule in which the work content is difficult to estimate, and rework is likely, Earned Value based schedule control systems should be considered', but notes that other factors, such as 'company culture, the nature of the project, and the competence of management' are also relevant to the choice (p. 87).

Globerson (1994) has investigated the way in which work breakdown structures (WBSs) influence the way in which projects are conceptualized. The WBS is a necessary prerequisite for critical path analysis, and since 'several possible patterns of WBS can be generated, despite the fact that all of them describe the same project' (p. 165), there are clearly serious implications here. Bachy and Hameri (1997) argue that 'the work breakdown structure is the backbone of the proper planning, execution and control of a project', and believe that the focus should be on this rather than on critical path models, as in traditional project scheduling. In particular, they argue that a 'product breakdown structure (PBS) is the absolute prerequisite for the design of a successful work breakdown structure' (p. 211).

Shtub (1997) has discussed the possibility of segmenting projects into subprojects, each of which is composed of the same set of activities. He argues that such segmentation is appropriate as a project management strategy when 'most project activities are very long compared to the length of the project, and precedence relations among activities are not simple', citing as an example 'road construction projects, where most activities are performed throughout the project'. Shtub explains: 'the size of the project segment is a decision variable. Thus CPM is a special case of the proposed models in which a single project segment exists. By increasing the number of project segments, better project plans can be developed and tighter controls can be exercised' (p. 18).

De Falco and Macchiaroli (1998) note that 'planning and monitoring play a major role as the cause of project failures', and discuss an approach to allocating the timing of monitoring and control activities more appropriately. Their approach builds on a critical path analysis framework.

Kotamaki and Hameri (1998) describe a computer-based system 'to build and maintain the schedules needed to manage time, resources, and progress in a large-scale and globally distributed project' (p. 27). The system was used to manage the construction of a complex large-scale particle detection system at the European Laboratory for Particle Physics (CERN) in Geneva, a project involving "more than 150 institutes, laboratories and companies from more than 35 countries" (p. 27). The project was decomposed into eight subprojects, each of which was further decomposed into between 200 to 300 work packages. Each work package could be considered as a project in its own right, and was decomposed into component activities and scheduled by its own manager. Coordination of the schedule of packages was managed by means of the World Wide Web. Kotamaki and Hameri comment that 'the system is more applicable to the construction phases of the subprojects than for the installation phase of the project, which requires a more centralised planning' (p. 33).

The research effort that continues to be expended in the area of critical path methods and associated approaches is impressive. Nevertheless, the reader may be forgiven the occasional moment of doubt as to its practical value. Maybe Krakowski (1974) was experiencing such a moment when he observed that Parkinson's Law, which states that work expands to fill the time available for it, indicates that slack in a network will tend to be used up, and that earlier activities will tend to consume slack at the expense of later activities.

6.3 Conclusion

Over the nearly fifty years since modern critical path analysis methods were first developed, they have evolved from cumbersome, specialist project management tools suitable for only the largest and most complex projects to flexible, easily-used, well-supported approaches which can and do contribute centrally to the management of projects of all sizes. Though some management scientists I have met have expressed irritation that critical path methods are no longer the preserve of specialists such as themselves, but are used routinely by project managers and others in their work, I view this, rather, as a measure of the success of the management science movement in contributing to the practice of management.

There is very much more to good project management than critical path networks. But a sound approach to scheduling project activities is still a core part of project management practice, and is likely to continue to be so for the foreseeable future. Critical path network approaches do this and will continue to provide this, though, as computing continues to advance in sophistication and intelligence, project managers and other users are likely to become more and more distanced from the techniques themselves, and, further, will be able to rely far more on the software to take on more of the planning and monitoring of projects should they wish to. To what extent these are good things is debatable. Though the provision of techniques to those who need them, in a form which they can use, is highly desirable, I am firmly convinced that an understanding of the underlying logic of the techniques is essential to their proper use in all but the most straightforward of contexts. The further notion of de-skilling the role of the project manager by relying on the decision-making capability of advanced project management software is disturbing, but the future need not be like that, and such a scenario should not stand in the way of the development of advanced software.

References

Adams, J.R. and Barndt, S.E. (1988). Behavioral implications of the project life cycle. In D.I. Cleland and W.R. King, *Project Management Handbook*, 2nd edn. New York: Van Nostrand Reinhold.

Anderson, D.R., Sweeney, D.J. and Williams, T.A. (1994) Project management: PERT/CPM. In D.R. Anderson, D.J. Sweeney and T.A. Williams, *An Introduction to Management Science*, 7th edn. St Paul, MI: West.

Bachy, G. and Hameri, A.-P. (1997). What to be implemented at the early stage of a large-scale project. *International Journal of Project Management*, 15, pp. 211–18.

Baker, B. (1996). Critical path analysis with a spreadsheet. *OR Insight*, 9:2, pp. 9-12.

Baker, B.N., Murphy, D.C. and Fisher, D. (1988). Factors affecting project success. In D.I. Cleland and W. R. King, *Project Management Handbook*, 2nd edn. New York: Van Nostrand Reinhold.

Boothroyd, H. (1978). *Articulate Intervention: The Interface of Science, Mathematics and Administration*. London: Taylor & Francis.

Callahan, M.T., Quackenbush, D.G. and Rowlings, J.E. (1991). *Construction Project Scheduling*. New York: McGraw-Hill.

Chapman, C.B., Cooper, D.F. and Page, M.J. (1987). Project planning and control. In C.B. Chapman, D.F. Cooper and M.J. Page, *Management for Engineers*. Chichester, UK: Wiley.

Chapman, C.B. and Ward, S.C. (1997). *Project Risk Management: Processes, Techniques and Insights*. Chichester, UK: Wiley.

Cho, J.G. and Yum, B.J. (1997). An uncertainty importance measure of activities in PERT networks. *International Journal of Production Research*, 35, pp. 2737–57.

Cleland, D.I. and King, W.R. (1988). *Project Management Handbook*, 2nd edn. New York: Van Nostrand Reinhold.

Cox, M.A.A. (1995). Simple Normal approximation to the completion time distribution for a PERT network. *International Journal of Project Management*, 13, pp. 265–70.

Dane, C.W., Gray, C.F. and Woodworth, B.M. (1979). Factors affecting the successful application of PERT/CPM systems in a government organization. *Interfaces*, 9:5, pp. 94–98.

Dawson, C.W. and Dawson, R.J. (1994). Clarification of node representation in generalized activity networks for practical project management. *International Journal of Project Management*, 12, pp. 81–88.

Dawson, R.J. and Dawson, C.W. (1998). Practical proposals for managing uncertainty and risk in project planning. *International Journal of Project Management*, 16, pp. 299–310.

De Falco, M. and Macchiaroli, R. (1998). Timing of control activities in project planning. *International Journal of Project Management*, 16, pp. 51–8.

Dodin, B.M. and Elmaghraby, S.E. (1985). Approximating the criticality indices of the activities in PERT networks. *Management Science*, 31, pp. 207–223.

Edwards, J.S. and Finlay, P.N. (1997). *Decision Making with Computers: The Spreadsheet and Beyond*. Pitman, London.

Gallagher, W. (1995). The *PC Direct* guide to buying project management software. *PC Direct*, December 1995, pp. 348–59.

Gallagher, W. (1997). The *PC Direct* guide to buying project management software. *PC Direct*, August 1997, pp. 494–506.

Gilbreath, R.D. (1988). Working with pulses, not streams: using projects to capture opportunity. In D.I. Cleland and W.R. King, *Project Management Handbook*, 2nd edn. New York: Van Nostrand Reinhold.

Globerson, S. (1994). Impact of various work-breakdown structures on project conceptualization. *International Journal of Project Management*, 12, pp. 165–71.

Gong, D. (1997). Optimization of float use in risk analysis-based network scheduling. *International Journal of Project Management*, 15, pp. 187–92.

Gong, D. and Hugsted, R. (1993). Time-uncertainty analysis in project networks with a new merge-event time-estimation technique. *International Journal of Project Management*, 11, pp. 165–74.

Gong, D. and Rowings, Jr, J.E. (1995). Calculation of safe float use in risk-analysis-oriented network scheduling. *International Journal of Project Management*, 13, 187–94.

Gordon, J. and Tulip, A. (1997). Resource scheduling. *International Journal of Project Management*, 15, pp. 359–70.

Hutchings, J.F. (1996). *CPM Construction Scheduler's Manual*. New York: McGraw-Hill.

Jaafari, A. (1996). Time and priority allocation scheduling technique for projects. *International Journal of Project Management*, 14, pp. 289–99.

Kayes, P. (1995). How ICL used project management techniques to introduce a new product range. *International Journal of Project Management*, 5, pp. 321–28.

Kidd, J.B. (1990). A comparison between the VERT program and other methods of project duration estimation. *Omega* 15, pp. 129–34.

Kidd, J.B. (1991). Project management. In S.C. Littlechild and M.F. Shutler (eds), *Operations Research in Management*. New York: Prentice Hall.

Klein, J.H. (1994). Cognitive processes and operational research: a human information processing perspective. *Journal of the Operational Research Society*, 45, pp. 855–66.

Kotamaki, M. and Hameri, A.-P. (1998). Planning and scheduling system for distributed, one-off and complex system projects. *Project Management*, 4:1, pp. 27–33.

Krakowski, M. (1974). PERT and Parkinson's Law. *Interfaces*, 5:1, 35–40.

Kuklan, H., Erdem, E., Nasri, F. and Paknedjad, M.J. (1993). Project planning and control: an enhanced PERT network. *International Journal of Project Management*, 11, 87–92.

Lang, D. W. (1977). *Critical Path Analysis*. 2nd edn. Sevenoaks, UK: Hodder & Stoughton.

Levin, R.I. and Kirkpatrick, C.A. (1966). *Planning and Control with PERT/CPM*. New York: McGraw-Hill.

Lock, D. (1996). *Project Management*, 6th edn. Aldershot, UK: Gower.

Lockyer, K. and Gordon, J. (1995). *Project Management and Project Network Techniques*. 6th edn. London: Financial Times/Prentice Hall.

Lowe, C.W. (1969). *Critical Path Analysis by Bar Chart: The New Role of Job Progress Charts*. London: Business Books.

Maroto, C. and Tormos, P. (1994). Project management: an evaluation of software quality. *International Transactions in Operational Research*, 1, pp. 209–21.

Maylor, H. (1999). *Project Management*, 2nd edn. London: Financial Times/Pitman Publishing.

Meredith, J.R. and Mantel Jr, S.J. (1995). *Project Management: A Managerial Approach*, 3rd edn. New York: Wiley.

Moder, J.J. (1988). Network techniques in project management. In D.I. Cleland and W.R. King (1988). *Project Management Handbook*, 2nd edn. New York: Van Nostrand Reinhold.

Moder, J.J., Phillips, C.R. and Davis, E.W. (1983). *Project Management with CPM, PERT and Precedence Diagramming*, 3rd edn. New York: Van Nostrand Reinhold.

Morris, P.W.G. (1994). *The Management of Projects*. London: Thomas Telford.

Mummolo, G. (1994). PERT-path network technique: a new approach to project planning. *International Journal of Project Management*, 12, pp. 89–99.

Mummolo, G. (1997). Measuring uncertainty and criticality in network planning by PERT-path technique. *International Journal of Project Management*, 15, pp. 377–87.

O'Brien, J.J. (1993). *CPM in Construction Management*. New York: McGraw-Hill.

Pritsker, A.A.B. (1968). GERT networks. *The Production Engineer*, October 1968.

Render, B. and Stair, Jr, R.M. (1994). Quantitative Analysis for Management, 3rd edn. Boston, MA: Allyn and Bacon.

Schonberger, R.J. (1981). Why projects are 'always' late: a rationale based on manual simulation of a PERT/CPM network. *Interfaces*, 11:5, pp. 66–70.

Schroeder, R.G. (1989). *Operations Management: Decision Making in the Operations Function.* New York: McGraw Hill.

Schtub, A. (1992). Evaluation of two schedule control techniques for the development and implementation of new technologies: a simulation study. *R&D Management,* 22, pp. 81–7.

Shtub, A. (1997). Project segmentation – a tool for project management. *International Journal of Project Management,* 15, pp. 15–19.

Shtub, A., Bard, J. F. and Globerson, S. (1994) *Project Management: Engineering, Technology and Implementation.* Englewood Cliffs, NJ: Prentice Hall.

Stott, D. (1998) The *PC Direct* Guide to buying project management software. *PC Direct,* June 1998, pp. 418–23.

Taha, H.A. (1987). *Operations Research: An Introduction,* 4th edn. New York: Collier Macmillan.

Targett, D. (1996). *Analytical Decision Making.* London: Pitman.

Turner, J.R. (1993). *The Handbook of Project-Based Management.* London: McGraw-Hill.

Van Gundy, A.B. (1988). *Techniques of Structured Problem Solving,* 2nd edn. New York: Van Nostrand Reinhold.

Wasil, E.A. and Assad, A.A. (1988). Project management on the PC: software, applications, and trends. *Interfaces,* 18:2, pp. 75–84.

Waters, C.D.J. (1991) *An Introduction to Operations Management.* Wokingham, UK: Addison Wesley.

Waters, C.D.J. (1989). *A Practical Introduction to Management Science.* Wokingham, UK: Addison Wesley.

Whittington, R., Pettigrew, A., Peck, S., Fenton, E. and Conyon, M. (1999). Change and complementarities in the new competitive landscape: a European panel study, 1992–1996. *Organization Science,* 10, 583–600

Williams, T.M. (1992). Practical use of distributions in network analysis. *Journal of the Operational Research Society,* 43, pp. 265–270.

Williams, T.M. (1993). What is critical? *International Journal of Project Management,* 11, pp. 197–200.

Williams, T.M. (1995). What are PERT estimates? *Journal of the Operational Research Society,* 46, pp. 1498–1504.

Winston, W.L. (1994). *Operations Research: Applications and Algorithms,* 3rd edn. Belmont, CA: Duxbury.

Woolsey, R.E.D. (1992). The fifth column: the PERT that never was or data collection as an optimizer. *Interfaces,* 22:3, pp. 112–14.

Exercises

In common with most other management science approaches, there are two aspects to knowledge of critical path network analysis. *Technical* knowledge is concerned with understanding and being able to employ the techniques. This is, generally, fairly straightforward to exercise and test: exercises can be well-formulated, and tend to have identifiable correct answers. *Practical* knowledge, on the other hand, is concerned with being able to use the techniques effectively in practice. For an applied discipline such as management science, it should be apparent that practical knowledge is essential: technical knowledge is of little use without it. Unfortunately, practical knowledge is much harder to exercise and test: real problems tend to be open-ended, with no identifiably unique correct answers. It is hard to set artificial problems for exercising practical, as opposed to technical skills. (The problem is, in fact, broader, and has consistently dogged the teaching of management science: technical skills are more straightforward to teach, and can be effectively taught within a standard classroom environment, while practical skills require some degree of experiential learning, dealing with real problems, that it is hard to create within the classroom.)

To address this problem, in this section readers are invited, first, to use the critical path network analysis techniques in contexts of their own choosing. There follows a technical exercise, with solution, for readers to test their technical ability.

Practical critical path network analysis exercise

Select a modestly-sized project, with which you are familiar, of your own choice. Suitable projects might include: home do-it-yourself projects; undergraduate or postgraduate projects; work-related projects or part-projects for which you have some degree of responsibility. Use critical path network analysis to model the project.

Initially, you will need to construct a work breakdown structure (WBS). You will have to decide to what level of detail you intend to model the project, and how many hierarchical levels it will contain. If you have access to a PC with critical path software, you can conduct a very much more detailed analysis, though it may not be necessary. If you are carrying out the analysis manually, I recommend that you restrict yourself to no more than about twenty activities.

You will have to decide on the scope of the project: what activities are part of the project, and therefore should be included in the model, and what activities are not, and should be left out. For example, if your project is to build a garden pond, you may feel that stocking the pond with plants and fish lies beyond the scope of the project you wish to analyse, or you may not.

If people other than yourself are involved in the project, it is useful to identify them at this stage. If there are specialist skills or resources which particular activities require, it is useful to identify them now, too.

Identify the precedence relationships between activities. Some relationships will be obvious; others less so. For example, in a student research project, it might be desirable not to start any research work until all the relevant literature has been read. But this might prove too lengthy, and you might therefore be prepared to start research after an initial reading of the literature. In this case you may wish to create two alternative models to compare. If you are using a PC, making such alterations on a 'what-if' basis is fairly quick and easy if you plan your model sensibly.

Estimate the durations of the activities. You may be happy to identify them deterministically, or you may wish to include uncertainty in your estimates by using the PERT approach. If you are including uncertainty, you may have to decide the scope of the uncertainty you wish to model. You may reckon that it will take between three and four weeks for you to carry out a particular piece of work, but does this allow for the possibility of illness during that time, or sudden other urgent demands on your time? Should it?

You are now in a position to employ the critical path techniques on the model you have constructed. Assemble a network diagram, identify the critical activities, and draw a Gantt chart. If appropriate, calculate the probability distribution of the project completion date. Investigate the possibility of reducing the duration of critical activities or the uncertainty associated with them (if any). Examine usage of resources, and consider the possible advantages of levelling or delaying resource usage. Identify suitable milestones in the project which you can use during the execution of the project to assess to what extent it is proceeding according to schedule.

It should be clear from the above that modelling even the simplest project requires many decisions that cannot be prescribed in advance. These decisions will be based on the particular context: what you are trying to achieve, and what assumptions you are prepared to make. It should also be clear that the modelling is likely to raise questions about the project that have hitherto not been addressed. As a result of the modelling, you may redesign the project. The direction of the modeller's attention to areas which he or she has not previously considered is one of the major benefits of modelling.

Technical critical path network analysis exercise: construction of a garden shed

We now turn to the consideration of technical skills. The following hypothetical project is sufficiently small to be analysed manually. Try it manually first, and, if possible, retry the analysis on a PC using critical path software.

Consider the following project: to erect a prefabricated garden shed. First of all, the construction needs to be planned: where in the garden the shed is to be placed, its orientation, and so on. The shed is to be built on a surface of stone paving slabs. Before these slabs, which will need to be obtained from a supplier, can be laid, the ground on which they are to be laid will have to be flattened. Once the slabs are laid, they must be left for a period of time. Then the shed itself, the parts of which must also be obtained from a (different) supplier, can be erected. The shed comprises four sides and a roof. Windows will be fitted in two of the sides, and a door in the third. Finally, an electric socket and light are to be fitted.

In the following tables I have listed the component activities in the shed construction project, together with other relevant data.

Component activities and numbering code

Activity number	Activity description
1	Plan
2	Flatten surface
3	Obtain stone
4	Lay foundations
5	Let foundations lie
6	Obtain materials
7	Prepare wood
8	Allow wood to dry
9	Erect sides
10	Fit windows
11	Fit door
12	Fit roof
13	Install electricity

Activity precedence relationships

Activity	Must be preceded by
1: Plan	–
2: Flatten surface	1
3: Obtain stone	1
4: Lay foundations	2, 3
5: Let foundations lie	4
6: Obtain materials	1
7: Prepare wood	6
8: Allow wood to dry	7
9: Erect sides	5, 8
10: Fit windows	9
11: Fit door	9
12: Fit roof	9
13: Install electricity	9

The table below lists the estimated durations of each of the activities, in hours.

Estimated durations for activities			
Activity	Estimated duration (hours)		
	optimistic	most likely	pessimistic
1: Plan	2	2	2
2: Flatten surface	2	2	2
3: Obtain stone	3	4	4
4: Lay foundations	3	4	6
5: Let foundations lie	8	8	12
6: Obtain materials	3	4	4
7: Prepare wood	3	3	3
8: Allow wood to dry	8	8	12
9: Erect sides	2	3	4
10: Fit windows	2	3	4
11: Fit door	1	2	3
12: Fit roof	2	3	4
13: Install electricity	3	4	6

Questions

Question 1: Assume (probably somewhat unrealistically) that the there is no bar to running activities in parallel where appropriate, because you will be able to call upon help, if necessary, from partner, friends or neighbours. Such help will make no difference to the duration of individual activities, however; only one person may work on each activity. Also assume (even less realistically) that work will continue non-stop until the job is finished: no overnight breaks, or breaks for meals or rests. (These assumptions will be dropped later.) Assume that the 'most likely' duration estimates are accurate (that is, ignore the 'optimistic' and 'pessimistic' estimates). Do the following:

(a) Construct A-O-N and A-O-A diagrams for the project.

(b) Assuming all activities start at the earliest times, find the earliest and latest start and finish times for each of the activities, find the amount of slack associated with each activity, identify the critical activities and the critical path, and find the total duration of the project.

(c) Draw a Gantt chart for the project.

Question 2. Now taking into account the 'optimistic' and 'pessimistic' duration estimates, conduct a PERT analysis of the project, repeating parts (b) and (c) of Question 1. In addition, find the durations for which there is a 1%, 10%, 25%, 50%, 75%, 90% and 99% probability, according to your analysis, of project completion within the specified duration.

Question 3. Now, assume that the project is to be started at 9.00 am on Day 1. Work will proceed until 1.00 pm, when a break of one hour, until 2.00 pm, will be taken. Work will then continue until 5.00 pm, when it will stop for the day. It will recommence the next day, when the same work pattern will be followed, and on subsequent days as necessary. Repeat parts (b) and (c) of Question 1, under this new assumption. Suggest any modifications to the work pattern you think might be sensible. (For this, and all subsequent questions, work solely with the 'most likely' duration estimates, as used in Question 1: do not revise the non-deterministic analysis of Question 2.)

Question 4. Repeat the analysis of Question 3 assuming you alone are working on the project, so that activities which require your labour cannot run in parallel.

Question 5. Returning to the analysis of Question 4, assume that only one person is available to assist you on the project, so that no more than two activities which require labour can run in parallel. Repeat the analysis of Question 4, taking this smoothing into account.

Solutions

Question 1 solution. The A-O-N diagram requires 13 nodes (one for each of the thirteen activities. The A-O-A diagram also requires 13 nodes (this is coincidence). Observing the convention that two or more activities may not span the same pair of nodes, a dummy activity is needed to distinguish between activities 2 and 3, and three dummy activities are required to distinguish between activities 10, 11, 12 and 13. From the A-O-A diagram, the following data can be derived:

Activity	Earliest start time (hours)	Earliest finish time (hours)	Latest start time (hours)	Latest finish time (hours)	Slack (hours)	Critical?
1	0	2	0	2	0	Yes
2	2	4	4	6	2	No
3	2	6	2	6	0	Yes
4	6	10	6	10	0	Yes
5	10	18	10	18	0	Yes
6	2	6	3	7	1	No
7	6	9	7	10	1	No
8	9	17	10	18	1	No
9	18	21	18	21	0	Yes
10	21	24	22	25	1	No
11	21	23	23	25	2	No
12	21	24	22	25	1	No
13	21	25	21	25	0	Yes

The critical path is the sequence of activities: 1–3–4–5–9–13. The duration of the project, in this unlikely scenario of non-stop work, is 25 hours. Activities 6, 7 and 8 share an hour of slack between them, while activities 10, 11, 12 and 13 can run in parallel, assuming you have three people to help you. These features become very clear when the Gantt chart is drawn.

Question 2 solution. Using the PERT formulae, the expected durations of the activities, and their variances and standard deviations, are as follows:

Activity	Expected duration (hours)	Variance (hours)^2	Standard deviation (hours)
1	2.00	0.00	0.00
2	2.00	0.00	0.00
3	3.83	0.03	0.17
4	4.17	0.25	0.50
5	8.67	0.44	0.67
6	3.83	0.03	0.17
7	3.00	0.00	0.00
8	8.67	0.44	0.67
9	3.00	0.11	0.33

Activity	Expected duration (hours)	Variance (hours)²	Standard deviation (hours)
10	3.00	0.11	0.33
11	2.00	0.11	0.33
12	3.00	0.11	0.33
13	4.17	0.25	0.50

These figures change the timings of the activities somewhat:

Activity	Earliest start time (hours)	Earliest finish time (hours)	Latest start time (hours)	Latest finish time (hours)	Slack (hours)	Critical?
1	0.00	2.00	0.00	2.00	0.00	Yes
2	2.00	4.00	3.83	5.83	1.83	No
3	2.00	5.83	2.00	5.83	0.00	Yes
4	5.83	10.00	5.83	10.00	0.00	Yes
5	10.00	18.67	10.00	18.67	0.00	Yes
6	2.00	5.83	3.17	7.00	1.17	No
7	5.83	8.83	7.00	10.00	1.17	No
8	8.83	18.67	10.00	18.67	1.17	No
9	18.67	21.67	18.67	21.67	0.00	Yes
10	21.67	24.67	22.84	25.84	1.17	No
11	21.67	23.67	23.84	25.84	2.17	No
12	21.67	24.67	22.84	25.84	1.17	No
13	21.67	25.84	25.84.	25.84	0.00	Yes

The expected duration of the project is now 25.84 hours, and the standard deviation of the critical path is 2.17 hours. This leads to the following estimated likelihoods of completion durations:

Probability that project will be complete	Duration (hours)
1%	20.78
10%	23.06
25%	24.39
50%	25.84
75%	27.29
90%	28.62
99%	30.90

In this case, the critical path, as indicated by the calculated expected durations, is the same as in Question 1. Note, however, that there is potential for the critical path to alter. For example, if the duration of activity 8 is towards the pessimistic estimate, while other durations remain close to their most likely estimates, the path 1–6–7–8–9–13 would become critical.

Question 3 solution. In repeating the analysis of Question 1, I have assumed that activities 5 and 8 (letting the foundations lie, and allowing the wood to dry) require no labour, and thus can continue during breaks or overnight. Other activities can take place only during designated working time. Under these assumptions, the project should take three days; it should be completed at 5.00 pm on the third day. This is not a surprising result given that there are now only seven working hours per day and the non-stop version of the project was scheduled to take 25 hours.

Study of the Gantt chart reveals that most of the second day is spent doing nothing except allowing the foundations to lie and the wood to dry. By finding an extra three working hours on the first day, these activities could take place overnight, and the project could be completed by 5.00 pm on the second day.

Question 4 solution. In this case, sticking rigidly to the allocated working hours means that the project will not be complete until 10 am on the sixth day.

Question 5 solution. In this case, sticking rigidly to the allocated working hours means that the project will not be complete until 12.00 mid-day on the fourth day.

There is, of course, considerable further scope for exploration of this project. For example, on the non-critical paths there is some scheduling flexibility, so schedules can be arranged to take into account convenience to some extent. If there is a cost associated with labour (which might be greater for working out of designated working hours), this can be traded off against the cost, if any, associated with the completion time of the project. If there is scope for reducing the duration of particular activities, but at a cost, then this can also be traded off against the cost associated with the completion time.

Index

Activity codes 122–3
  hierarchical structuring 162
Activity duration 113
  average 135
  mean value 136
  uncertainty 134
Activity timing 127–30
Activity-on-arrow (AOA) network
  diagram 126–7, 129, 132
  computer displays 151
Activity-on-node (AON) network
  diagram 124–5
  computer displays 151
Algorithm development 91–2
  hybrid 91
Aluminium recycling *see*
  Arabian Light Metals
  Company (ALMC)
Arabian Light Metals Company
  (ALMC), LP application 3, 4,
  82–4
Artificial variables 43–8

Basic variables 33, 64–5
Binding constraints 18
Blending/mixing, LP application
  88
Brunswick Smelting, Canada, LP
  application 79–82

CA Superproject (Computer
  Associates software) 149
Canonical primal 53
  transformation rules 53–4
Computer software 67, 75–6
  for AOA diagramming 151
  for AON diagramming 151
  CA Superproject 149

  for complex scheduling 144,
    148, 161
  for critical path networks
    149–55
  ease of use 150
  graphical displays 150–51
  LINDO 67, 92
  Lotus 123 spreadsheet package
    155
  Microsoft Excel Solver 67–71
  MS Project 149
  multi-user compatability 153–4
  Primavera Project Planner 149
  project planning packages 119
  for resource scheduling 151–2
  selecting 154–5, 161
  Supertrak Project Manager 149
  Windows-based 150
  XPRESS-MP 71–5
Constraints 9
  binding 18
  'equal to' form 62, 63
  equality 48
  graphing 10–12
  'greater than or equal to' form
    60–62, 63
  'less than or equal to' form
    57–60, 63
  non-binding 18
  non-negativity 10
  redundant 28
  use of sensitivity analysis 19–21
Crash duration 140
Crashing solution method 91–2
Critical path, definition 130
Critical path method (CPM) 120,
  159
  appropriate application 163–4

benefits 121, 132, 158, 160
costing 162
origins 157
use of spreadsheets 155–6
Critical path network analysis
119–20
practical exercise 179–81
technical exercise 181–7

Data envelopment analysis (DEA)
90
Decision-making units (DMUs) 90
Delta Air Lines, LP application
3–4
Denim jeans manufacture,
worked example 7–8
Dual problem 49–53
Dual value *see* Opportunity cost
Dummy activities 130–31
Duration *see* Activity duration
Duration/cost, trade-off 140–43

Earliest finish (EF) time 127
Earliest start (ES) time 127
EBSP Detector Project (example)
121–5, 137–8, 143
Equality constraints 48

Feasible area, graphical solution
11–12
Financial problems, LP
application 88
Free slack 130

Gantt charts 110, 112, 132–4
benefits 116–17
compiling 113–14
computer displays 151
Goal programming 89–90
Graphical Evaluation and Review
Technique (GERT) 164
Graphical solution method 7,
10–15
interpreting results 16–17

procedure 16

Health Service, Rome, LP
application 3, 4
Hybrid algorithms 91

Infeasible problems 27
Integer linear programming (ILP)
89
Interior point solution methods 91
Iso-line 13
Iso-profit line 13

Labour cost profiles 145, 146
Labour scheduling, LP application
88
Latest finish (LF) time 128
Latest start (LS) time 128
Latest time schedule 145
Life-cycle *see* Project life-cycle
LINDO (computer LP package)
67, 92
Linear programming
application examples 77–84
common features 85–6
development 4–5
specialist applications 87–8

Marginal approach 19
Marketing and media, LP
application 88
Mathematical programming
models 4–5, 89–90
Microsoft Excel Solver (computer
LP package) 67–71
Milestones 116
Minimization problems 24–6
changes in constraints 63
objective functions 54
sensitivity analysis 63
Minimum time schedule 142–3
Modelling
developments 92
limitations 85–6

number of activities 161
program benefits 73–5
use of subscript notation 83
MS Project (Microsoft computer
software) 149

Net present value (NPV) 145
Networks 109
analysis techniques 119–20
Non-basic variables 33, 65
Non-binding constraints 18
Non-linear programming 90
Non-negativity constraint 10
Normal distribution 138–40
standard 139

Objective function (OF) 8–9
graphing 13–14
minimization transformation 54
sensitivity analysis 21–4, 63–5
Opportunity costs 20–21, 57
Optimization
graphical method 14–15
using spreadsheets 67–71

Pivot column 36, 40
Pivot element 36, 39, 41
Pivot row 36, 39, 40–41
Planning, stages 159
Precedence relationships 123–4
Primal problem 49–53
transforming to dual 53
Primal-dual relationship, key
properties 51–3
Primavera Project Planner
(computer software) 149
Probability distributions
Beta 134–5
normal 138–40
spread *see* Standard deviation
Problem formulation 10
Production possibility frontier 11
Production scheduling, LP
application 87

Profit line 13, 21, 22–4
Profit maximization, use of
sensitivity analysis 56–60
Project activities 111, 113, 114–15
Project evaluation and review
technique (PERT) 120, 134, 161
costing 162
limitations 158, 162
Project risk analysis 164
Projects
costing 116
duration variance 137
generic features 110–12
life-cycle 158–60
management 108, 153, 157
milestones 116
scope 107–108
use of specialized software 161

Redundant constraints 28
Reporting developments 92
Resource allocation/product mix,
LP application 87
Resource constraints 144
Resource delaying 144–5
Resource levelling 143–4
Resource scheduling 164
computer software 151–2
Resource usage 143–7
monitoring 146–7

Santos seaport, Brazil, LP
application 77–9
Schedule graphs *see* Gantt charts
Sensitivity analysis 5, 56
changes in constraints 56–62
changes in objective function
63–5
simple 17–18
use on constraints 19–21
use on objective function 21–4
using spreadsheets 71
Shadow price *see* Opportunity
cost

Simplex solution method 66, 91
  dual problem 49–55
  extensions 41–8
  formulation 30–31
  minimization problems 48
  process 31–40
  summary 40–41
  use of artificial variables 43–8
  use of surplus variables 41–2
Simplex tableaux 32, 33, 38, 39, 44, 45, 46, 47
  transforming steps 36–8
Simultaneous equations, using 19
Slack 130
Slack variables 30–31
Solution algorithm development 91–2
Spreadsheets
  Lotus 123 package 155
  for optimization 67–71
  use in critical path network applications 155–6
  see also Computer software
Standard deviation 136
Statistical independence 136
Subscript notation, use in modelling 83
Supertrak Project Manager (Primavera computer software) 149

Surplus variable 41–2

Total slack 130
Trimloss/cutting stock problems, LP application 88

Unbounded problems 28

Variables
  artificial 43–8
  basic 33, 64–5
  non-basic 33, 65
  slack 30–31
  surplus 41–2
Variance, as measure of distribution spread 136
Venture Evaluation and Review Technique (VERT) 164

Warm start solution method 91–2
What-if analysis *see* Sensitivity analysis
Work breakdown structure (WBS) 121–3, 159

XPRESS-MP (computer LP package) 71–5, 92
  model builder 72–4
  optimizer 72, 74–5